"Because I am passionate about doing all I can to bring about a greater human connection, I believe in the value of huddles. Designed to create engagement, conversations, storytelling, self-improvement, discovery, and more, an intelligent huddle can help us meet our basic human need for connection and communication.

Just because we're face-to-face with people does not mean we connect with them. And just because we're meeting virtually does not mean it's impossible to connect. By following Andrea's wisdom and mentoring, we can all master the context of a huddle, the words to use, the energy needed, and the step-by-step formula to bring out the best dialogues for success.

Using Andrea's beautiful guidance will help any team, family, or group discover the rich value of huddles. Well done, Andrea!"

—Winn Claybaugh
Dean and Co-Owner of Paul Mitchell Schools
Author, *Be Nice (Or Else!)*

"As a leader, I know that focusing on leveraged activities is essential to building a successful business. One of these activities is holding effective, daily huddles. Using the principles in Andrea's book, Intelligent Huddles, our daily huddles and key educational metrics have significantly improved. Intelligent Huddles successfully breaks down the 'why and how' of holding effective huddles. I encourage anyone looking to improve the connection, unity, and focus of their organization to read Intelligent Huddles."

—Lou Starita
Dean, Paul Mitchell The School
Boise, Nampa, Provo, Richland, Spokane & Twin Falls

"Intelligent Huddles is a brilliant template for creating great communication and alignment for any company. Build or enhance your company's foundation by actively putting Intelligent Huddles to work. Thank you, Andrea, for the passion and dedication to this labor of love that has taken my businesses to new heights."

—**Shawn Trujillo**
Co-founder, Lunatic Fringe Salons
Owner, Paul Mitchell the School, Salt Lake City

"I have been a business owner most of my life and I've never seen a system generate positive changes in an organization quite like Andrea Hemmer's Intelligent Huddles. Andrea provides a step-by-step plan that helps leaders implement a process to drive real growth and team unity. This book is a game-changer for any leader."

—**Tommy Ahlquist, MD**
CEO, Ball Ventures Ahlquist

"Drea Hemmer is a woman in the trenches who has discovered how to develop success within a team-based culture. Using inspiration, creativity, and business intelligence, she distills in this book her secrets for growing people. It is a must read if you lead a team of any sort. Her huddle system is the business edge you've been looking for."

—**Lyn Christian**
Owner, SoulSalt Inc.,
Master Certified Coach (ICF MCC)

"Drea has written a must-read primer for anyone wanting to grow their business. The practical steps can be used immediately to grow your business and get results. Read this book and learn from one of the best!"

—**Andrea Lang**
Salon and Paul Mitchell Schools Owner

INTELLIGENT HUDDLES

Copyright © 2021 by Andrea Hemmer

All rights reserved.

No part of this book may be reproduced or transmitted in any form or by any means, electronic or mechanical, including photocopying, recording, or by any information storage and retrieval system, without written permission from the publisher. For all inquiries please contact Innovator Press at www.InnovatorPress.com.

ISBN (paperback) 979-8-9851902-0-5
ISBN (ebook) 979-8-9851902-1-2
Library of Congress Control Number: 2021950404

Ghostwriter & Lead Editor: Kevin Mullani
Cover & Interior Design: Innovator Press
www.InnovatorPress.com

Line Edits: Kevin Anderson & Associates
www.ka-writing.com

Parts of the content presented in this book are adapted from **Conversational Intelligence**® and the work of Judith E. Glaser.
www.creatingwe.com

Printed in the United States

INTELLIGENT HUDDLES

How to Launch and Facilitate Meaningful
Daily Huddles to Improve Team
Communication, Strengthen Culture,
and Reduce Employee Turnover

ANDREA HEMMER

INNOVATOR
PRESS

CONTENTS

FOREWORD ix

INTRODUCTION 1

CHAPTER 1
    SO, WHAT'S THE PROBLEM? 13

CHAPTER 2
    BASICS OF NEUROSCIENCE 29

CHAPTER 3
    APPLYING NEUROSCIENCE 43

CHAPTER 4
    IT STARTS WITH YOU 55

CHAPTER 5
    FINAL PREPARATION: SCHEDULES, SPACE, & THE HUDDLE AGENDA 69

CHAPTER 6
    THE ART OF RUNNING AN INTELLIGENT HUDDLE 87

CHAPTER 7
    MEASURING HUDDLE SUCCESS 103

CHAPTER 8
    CONCLUSION 119

ACKNOWLEDGEMENTS

I have so much gratitude in my heart and want to acknowledge and thank the people in my circle who made this book possible. It was an effort by many amazing people and I could not have accomplished this without such an incredible team.

I want to start by thanking my talented, supportive publisher, Kevin Mullani, at Innovator Press. His guidance, dedication, efforts, and partnership were exactly what I needed to bring my book into reality.

Thank you to my business partners, Shawn Trujillo and Angie Katsanevas, for always believing in me and supporting me. I am grateful that you gave me the opportunity to become a leader.

I have to give a heartfelt thank you to my coach, Lyn Christin, who has helped me see through the impossible to what is possible.

Thank you to my incredible team at Lunatic Fringe Salon in Boise for believing in the huddle and showing up each day. Our consistent practice planted the seed for this book. I am so grateful for all the team members that have been a part of this journey over the past decade.

Thank you, Neil Ducoff, for all of your love, support, and care. I may never have the words to express how honored I am to have you be a part of this journey and the gratitude I have for your foreword. I have always had a dream to partner with those who share my passion to support other leaders and team cultures. You have showed many ways to do this with the services you and your team provide at Strategies.com and I hope this book support your efforts.

Thank you from the bottom of my heart to all of all the incredible leaders, friends, and business owners that endorsed this book.

Thank you for your support by reading this book! Your continued support through recommendations and reviews allows me to reach the leaders and business owners that will benefit from this message the most.

Thank you to my friends and family, I have been so blessed to have you all in my life and pushing me to always do my best.

I must share my biggest heartfelt thank you to two of the most influential, loving people in my life—my biggest support team and believers in me—my Mom and Dad. I was so blessed to have wonderful, loving parents that taught me that anything I put my heart and mind to is possible. My dad is my greatest teacher. He has taught me the importance of "slowing down," being present, and living life to the fullest. I am forever grateful for his wisdom and love.

And last, I have to express infinite gratitude for my incredible husband, Levi. You always support my wildest ideas and dreams. You are the love of my life and without this love, partnership, and support, this big dream of mine would not have become a reality. Thank you so much Levi! I love you!

FOREWORD

by Neil Ducoff

Winning in business isn't just about providing great products or services to your customers. It's about hitting monthly goals and creating bottom line **net profit**.

In an employee-based business, creating net profit isn't just "money for the owner," it's money that funds growth, allows for payroll increases, pays back loans, and much more. But net profit doesn't happen by accident. It must be planned and coordinated. Simply put, creating business growth and net profit is all about coordinated teamwork—which means achieving that often elusive state where everyone is "on the same page."

My name is Neil Ducoff, founder of www.strategies.com, a business coaching and training company for salons and spas. I've been coaching owners for over 40 years and the question I hear more than any other is, "How do I get everyone on the same page?"

I'm also the guy you'll read about in this book that led the seminar Andrea Hemmer attended and first heard about the importance of doing daily huddles. Like most business owners, Andrea's initial reaction to doing daily huddles was, "This will never work in my business!" Until, of course, she tried them and changed her business forever.

If you are a business owner that wants everyone on the same page, wants a dynamic team-based culture, wants to set their team up to win monthly goals … and create net profit … daily huddles are a no-brainer.

OK, so as daily huddles are starting to make sense — then come the inherent huddle "yeah but" questions:

- Yeah but … how can huddles work when everyone starts their work day at different times?
- Yeah but … are huddles mandatory for all employees?
- Yeah but … what can we truly accomplish in a short daily huddle?
- Yeah but … will everyone show up for huddle?
- Yeah but … how do I keep everyone engaged and not get bored?
- Yeah but … if huddles are mandatory, do I have to pay them to be at huddle?
- Yeah but … who does the huddle if I'm not there?

Rest assured, all of these questions have an answer. The key is not to get yourself stuck in "yeah but" land.

Making daily huddles work in your organization begins with your commitment to start <u>and stay</u> the course. Missing even one huddle is a leadership compromise because it breaks trust in you and your leadership. Daily huddles are not a "kind of/sort of" type of event. Remember, if you want everyone on the same page … you have to be a consistent leader and use a proven system of effective communication. *Intelligent Huddles* provides that system and will absolutely keep the important information flowing.

Foreword

Andrea's book, *Intelligent Huddles*, is a beautifully written game plan that shows leaders and business owners how daily huddles can improve any company. You'll learn how to schedule, organize content, deliver and keep your huddles engaging, and most of all, consistent.

FACT: You can't win the business game if your team doesn't know the goal, doesn't know the score, and doesn't know if they're winning or losing.

And that brings us back to the absolute importance of learning, implementing, and mastering daily huddles in your company.

Once you begin doing consistent daily huddles, you will discover what every leader before you has discovered — daily huddles ROCK!

- Daily huddles get and keep everyone on the same page.
- Daily huddles inspire higher levels of teamwork.
- Daily huddles create consistency and predictability in your company.
- Daily huddles tighten your culture.
- And, daily huddles help create wins and bottom line **net profit**.

So, don't read this book to decide if you want to implement daily huddles in your company. Read this book to learn a proven system that can help your team and company achieve its full potential.

—Neil Ducoff
Founder, www.strategies.com

INTRODUCTION

Is the culture within your company strong enough that you could lock your doors for 53 days, then reopen them without losing a single member of your team? Is your team's communication effective enough that you could implement safety guidelines that have never been employed before in a matter of hours?

Like thousands of businesses across America, this was exactly what I had to do in March 2020 when the Idaho governor announced, "All businesses and government agencies must cease non-essential operations at physical locations across Idaho." As a high-end salon, we were considered non-essential and forced to close our doors for an unknown amount of time.

Despite facing an uncertain future, I felt like I had an advantage over most businesses. I knew we had an incredibly strong culture in our company that created loyal, problem-solving professionals. I knew we had a solid and consistent platform for communication that created clarity and unity among team members. I had peace of mind, even during a crisis, because I knew we could reopen with minimal impact on our operation and team efficiency.

After being closed for 53 days, we finally got the word on Friday, May 25 that we could reopen as soon as we put new safety guidelines in place. Thanks to incredible communication that got everyone on the same page quickly, we opened the following Monday. In fact, if you walked into our salon that first morning back, you would have witnessed everyone working in sync, as if we had all been operating this way for years. Possibly even more remarkable was that every single employee returned happily to work.

> *Despite facing an uncertain future, I felt like I had an advantage over most businesses.*

So what made this possible? Why did the young professionals that work at our salon love it so much that they didn't want to leave, even when our doors were locked? How were we able to communicate so effectively that we were able to open in a matter of hours, when other salons took several days?

This was all possible because we do a daily huddle.

Twelve years ago, I never could have imagined that twelve minutes per day could create amazing business growth, rock-steady culture, strong communication, and relationships that foster support and teamwork. Especially since we opened our salon during one of the worst economic times in history.

STYLIST TO SALON OWNER

I started my journey as a business owner in the fall of 2008, which was a very unsettling time to start a business of any kind. Not only were we opening the doors during a period some have compared to the Great Depression, but Boise had not been introduced to the type of upscale salon experience we were bringing to the city at that time. Even though the timing wasn't perfect, being a team member at the Lunatic Fringe salon in Utah helped me realize I wanted to open a business that provided the same type of culture, systems, and support.

Introduction

Ever since graduating from the Paul Mitchell School in 2000, I wanted to work in an environment that resonated with my own values that could also ensure a viable career in the beauty industry. The salon I worked in right out of school did not meet these criteria, so I was always keeping my eye out for a better fit. I noticed Lunatic Fringe initially because the name caught my attention, but when I started to research the company it was very obvious that it represented the type of business I wanted to be a part of.

Lunatic Fringe focused on a five-star guest experience in addition to the services typically found in most salons. Guests always appeared to leave happy, even though the cost was high. This was intentional as it attracted people that wanted the best out of their experience— and Lunatic Fringe delivered just that.

The stylists were not only successful, but they were extremely well educated and were absolute professionals in their craft. They also seemed to really love working for Lunatic Fringe, which told me the organization had good leadership and a great culture. Also, the salon itself was very well-kept and it was clear they took pride in constantly evolving to keep up with current trends and best practices. So, I applied to be a stylist and was blessed to begin a new journey in a culture where I could thrive, surrounded by supportive leadership and team members.

I loved the culture, the systems, the core values and beliefs of the company, and the innovation and support within the organization. The leadership at Lunatic Fringe created an environment where I felt a strong sense of belonging and like-mindedness that helped me believe anything was possible—including opening my own location.

After working at Lunatic Fringe in Utah for three years, my husband, Levi, and I decided to move to Boise to be closer to his family. I knew I could not leave behind the elements of Lunatic Fringe that I had grown to love so much, so we decided to bring it with us. Levi had a business degree and I quickly developed as a leader at the salon so we knew we were up to the challenge of opening a new location. Working closely with the founders, Shawn Trujillo and Angie Katsanevas, we developed a plan and put the idea in motion.

I continued to work in Salt Lake City while preparing the new location in Boise, traveling back and forth almost every other week. I worked seven days a week from the end of 2006 until we officially opened the doors in 2008. It was a lot of hard work and long days, but the vision of opening my own Lunatic Fringe salon was finally a reality, despite the troubled economy.

I have always been a highly optimistic, solution-driven person, so I often said, "The great thing about starting a business at a time like this is there is nowhere to go but up." As I reflect back and connect the dots in my life, I see very clearly how I became a leader, doing the work that I love.

I grew up in a very small town with a population of less than 1,500 people in central Utah. I am certain it isn't any bigger today. I am a middle child with four other siblings, so I always had to work to stand out in one way or another. My parents stayed married until the day my dad suddenly passed away, and my home was very loving and filled with a lot of energy, business, and support.

I had a lot of energy as a child and rarely sat still, so my parents enrolled me in a lot of different sports to keep me busy. Little did I know how many lessons I would take from being involved in team and individual sports. Even though I excelled in all of them, team sports really spoke to me in a deep way. They fulfilled my love of being surrounded by people, learning a game of purpose, strategy, winning and losing, and all the other great qualities being on a team can teach you. I loved the friendships, support, and celebrating wins with others. Even then, I loved the energy of huddles and receiving guidance from the coach. Everything about being part of a team spoke to me, and still does. I always knew I could go further with a team than on my own and I always had a natural interest in being the leader.

Another part of my sports experience that was key to my development was being coached by great and not-so-great leaders. I have been a part of team huddles that were uplifting, efficient, valuable, and full of support. And I've been a part of huddles that offered nothing but negativity and yelling from the coach, pointing out all the things we were doing as team that wasn't working. I felt the negative impact it made when we would go back on the field, just as I've felt it in business.

Growing up in a small town is very much at the root of who I am and I see it show up more and more in my life. I love being part of a community and part of a family bigger than what my home can hold. I also know a huge part of what makes me me was having a great teacher like my dad. He helped establish strong core values of energy, hope, success, and freedom that drive me to always be the best leader I can be. And early on in my business, I needed these values to keep me moving forward.

EARLY DAYS OF LEADERSHIP

I remember my early days of leadership. I had a vision of seeing the business I had just opened filled with team members and clients. As a new leader and business owner, I was running the show and was the only person who knew what needed to be done to make each day a success. I had team members that needed important information, clients that had to be taken care of, ordering to do, cleaning, stocking … the list goes on and on.

As I got into each day, I started to see a pattern of certain things happening over and over. I found myself running from team member to team member saying the same things. I knew there had to be a more efficient way to share information that would create more growth each day, strengthen our team, and help support me as the leader. I was searching for a solution to eliminate the chaos that constantly ate up time and drained my energy; chaos that created negative energy among the team, was not supportive, and even drove many to leave.

> *I knew there had to be a more efficient way to share information that would create more growth each day, strengthen our team, and help support me as the leader.*

"How do I do this?" I would ask myself over and over. I felt like the ball in a pinball machine, flying from one team member to the next. I was delivering information in a very reactive way, and lots of things would be lost in translation. There was often confusion as to why a person hadn't followed through on my instructions, and why there were so many missed opportunities. My team was weak and the business was not growing. The craziest thing is, I was given the answer early on. I just didn't think it was *the* answer.

The year before we opened our salon, my husband and I attended a workshop for new salon owners. The man conducting the workshop, Neil Ducoff, was a very successful business consultant and coach for large, Fortune 500 companies as well as small businesses. The part of the workshop that really stuck with me was when he talked about the importance of *daily* huddles. I thought to myself, no way would I ever do huddles *every* morning. I actually thought it sounded kind of cheesy. I was a resister and left the workshop believing they were not worth the effort.

A few months after opening our salon, my days would go something like this: I would be the first to arrive. I would connect with my husband, who was running all the front-end operations, the books, and basically the "business" side of the business at the time. He would let me know important information that I needed to share with the team. Then, I would be cut loose to try and get that information to the entire team, only catching them in fleeting moments, one by one, if I was lucky. Some days I would find a way to get the information to them, other days I would hope it was passed along to them correctly. This could be anything from products that were on back order to letting team members know somebody was out sick—which was a big deal when that person was scheduled to provide support in places where the most help was needed.

I was the person being told everything and then left to figure it out. Day after day, I felt like all I was doing was running around putting out fires. I was the only one coming up with solutions to problems, and left the salon each day totally exhausted.

Another problem was that there was no time for group acknowledgements or celebrations. Again, it was just me trying to find a space to squeeze in this very important piece of team-building. I really wasn't building relationships and neither my team nor I were very productive. Of course, some days were better than others as far as feeling like we were united, but those were sporadic at best.

One morning, I was thinking about what changes needed to be made so I could have a better understanding of the people I worked with. I wondered how we could start to communicate efficiently and better understand where we could all contribute to a common goal. What could we do to create a sense of belonging, which is very important to all human beings? How could I feel more supported in sharing the daily challenges and victories?

And then, in what seemed like a loud voice I heard the words, "DAILY HUDDLE!" I finally realized the purpose of a daily huddle. My thoughts circled and I wondered, *What if I could talk to my team every day and feel connected and supported? How much time would I be willing to spend each morning if I knew I didn't have to run people down all throughout the day, or send separate messages to each team member and find time to go back and forth with them?* My mind was made up. I didn't know exactly how, but I knew I had to make it happen. The next day we started the ritual that has become the main component of our team and business success.

We haven't missed a morning huddle since the day we started. Even while we were closed during the quarantine, we still did a team huddle every day on-line. Speaking with my team members later, many of them said the huddles were the main thing they looked forward to each day. They gave them inspiration and a reason to be hopeful. We kept the culture of support and love alive, even when we weren't able to be together, and not a single stylist quit.

How does this translate into numbers you care about? According to thesalonbusiness.com, the total annual revenue for 257,000 salons and barbershops in the US is $63 billion.[1] This means the average annual revenue for a hair salon business is $245,000. Sam, one of my coaching clients, runs a salon in Salt Lake and has been utilizing huddles for almost a year. Like us, he had to lock his doors due to the pandemic but continued to do daily huddles. Just three weeks after reopening, he and his small team exceeded $200,000 in revenue. Not only is this an incredible number, but Sam achieved this while limited to only ten people in the salon at one time! Now that they are back to capacity, they are bringing in $300,000 per month. Sam credits much of this success to huddles and is proud to report his team's culture is strong, turnover is very low, and the team is bursting with determination, creativity, and drive.

Sam also shared that he and Shawn Trujillo, Co-founder and CEO of Lunatic Fringe, recently had a phone call with the CEO of one of the biggest hair care companies in the US—an internationally recognized brand. The CEO asked how the salons were doing coming out of quarantine. Sam shared the success both of our salons were having and how smooth the transition had been for the teams. The

Introduction

CEO was taken aback and let him know these results were not the case for the vast majority of salon owners he had reached out to.

This was a huge victory for Sam, so I asked him what he believed kept his team together and made it possible to have this level of success? He answered, "It's going to sound silly, but you know what it was? It was our daily huddles. I thought about doing them once a week, or every other day. I wondered how we could possibly have something to say to each other every day during quarantine. But I just knew we had to do them every day, and that is what kept my team together and made it possible to come back strong." Once the salon reopened, Sam's team thanked him for keeping the huddles going during the time they were away. This brought a big smile to my face. It was a beautiful testimonial and is exactly why I'm so passionate about sharing this information with other businesses.

It may be easy to dismiss the daily huddle and believe it only works in the salon industry, but could never work in your organization. This couldn't be further from the truth! The process that I'm going to teach you in this book works for any team. It is not tied to a specific business. Rather, it is built on team-building principles designed to create high productivity, a positive emotional environment, and effective communication. I guarantee my system for daily huddles is different than anything you've tried before. I have integrated science on how the brain works as well as communication techniques that are scientifically proven to be more effective. I call my version Intelligent Huddles™, and the information in this book will be a key component of your team's ongoing success.

This book will provide the step-by-step action plan you need to implement Intelligent Huddles™ with your team. After building a foundation of knowledge about huddles and some of the science behind what makes the brain work, the first couple of steps are all about preparing you as the leader to bring this new concept to your team. Next, I'll cover the specific elements required to plan a huddle agenda that never gets stale. I'll show you how to determine if huddles are making a difference in your business—including specific metrics to track—and what to do if the huddles aren't working. I'll show you how to level up your team so you can teach senior leaders to also run huddles, freeing you to run other aspects of your business. Finally, I'll walk you through my proprietary CONNECT technique to run each huddle for maximum efficiency and productivity.

I understand that there is a lot of fear that shows up when beginning something new, or creating change in a work environment. Don't worry, I am here to guide you through it all. There are plenty of personal stories from my own business, and business owners I have consulted, that relay how we got over barriers and personal false beliefs. Barriers such as getting your senior team onboard with the new plan, what to do when team members show up at different times of day, how to come up with fresh topics every day so huddles don't get stale, and what to do differently to ensure success, even if you've tried daily meetings before and they didn't work.

What leader doesn't want to see their team become one with unity, clarity, appreciation and understanding of how each person can contribute in large and small ways? An Intelligent Huddle™ is the magic sauce that spreads the energy every leader wants to be spreading throughout their environments every day.

Imagine what being able to effectively communicate with your team daily can do for your productivity. Imagine how much easier it will be to provide positive guidance to your team when you have a basic understanding of how the mind works. Imagine utilizing an entire team to solve problems instead of being solely responsible for fixing it all. Imagine how nice it will be when challenges that you currently face with your team and your culture become opportunities to grow instead of pains that keep you awake at night ... all because of a ritual that only takes twelve to fifteen minutes per day!

Introduction

This is not a fantasy world that only exists in the space of our dreams. This is real. This is totally possible and much easier than you think! So turn the page and start building strong communication, a rock-steady culture, relationships that foster support and teamwork, and create the amazing growth that you have been dreaming about for your business.

CHAPTER 1

So, What's The Problem?

I knew something in my business needed to change. The way I was currently working would not be sustainable over time. I was becoming exhausted in my leadership. I was chasing people down each day, waiting for them to walk through the door to get my urgent messages to them. I would email team members, then wonder if they got the email. Before they could respond, I would send a text telling them to check their email, eventually pouncing on them as soon as they arrived for work—which is never a good time to bring anyone into a reactive message! By reactive message I mean, it was usually charged with emotion and could very easily incite an undesirable emotion or reaction from the recipient. It was all draining valuable time and energy that I should have been dedicating to key areas to grow my business.

When I would put time into finding a solution, the thought of having daily huddles would pop up, but I quickly chased it away with all the reasons why it would be too hard, how it would be one more thing that I would have to plan, and that my team would never go for it. It was all very exhausting, and I am sure you can relate.

My exhaustion was just the tip of the iceberg, however. There were serious issues in my business that I knew were there, but that I thought were too big to be fixed by something as small as a daily meeting. If I had to tag one thing as the problem, I would say it was poor communication. I could see that on the surface, but what I didn't realize was how much of my business, and my ability to run my company, was really being affected.

The same set of problems are not only universal across industries, but can all be remedied with the same tool.

Before I can go deep into exactly how to implement my system, I need everyone to understand that the same set of problems are not only universal across industries, but can all be remedied with the same tool—the Intelligent Huddle™. By the time you finish this chapter, you will have a complete picture of the most common problems caused by not having daily huddles, the reasons leaders may have abandoned daily meetings in the past, and why my method is different than anything they've tried before. Let's start by exploring how problems like team member turnover, poor culture, and ineffective communication are more intimately related than typically thought.

TEAM MEMBER TURNOVER

I have worked in the salon business for twenty years and one issue that plagues the beauty industry more than most is team member turnover. The Bureau of Labor Statistics shows the personal care industry has one of the shortest tenures for team members, with an average of 3.1 years.[1] If they would break it down further, I'm pretty sure stylists at salons average quite a bit less than that. Salons aren't the only businesses with team member turnover as a problem, however. Other industries, such as technology (software), finance and insurance, hospitality, and healthcare all struggle as well. Constantly replacing team members, especially fully trained and qualified team members, can be a severe blow to revenue.

According to Gallup, a global consulting firm that specializes in culture transformation and organizational effectiveness, the cost of replacing an individual team member can range from one-half to two times their annual salary.[2] Considering the money required to advertise for a position, time spent during the interview, hiring, and training process, and the productivity cost of losing an experienced worker, it's not hard to see how the expense of losing a team member adds up quickly. But the impact isn't just financial. If you lose one of your more talented team members, it can cause serious damage to morale and productivity from other workers. All for a problem that doesn't have to exist.

The cost of replacing an individual team member can range from one-half to two times their annual salary.

Gallup also states that "fifty-two percent of voluntarily exiting team members say their manager or organization could have done something to prevent them from leaving their job."[3] Something as simple as frequent conversations about what matters to them can have a tremendous effect. An ongoing survey by Peakon titled *The Employee Voice* has collected nearly 11 million responses from workers about job satisfaction. The top three answers to the open-ended question, "If you had a magic wand, what's the one thing you would change about your organization?" were pay, communication, and manager/staff relationships.[4] While pay may not be something you can easily accommodate, opening lines of communication and training managers to be engaged, caring leaders should be achievable. Engaged, caring leaders create engaged team members, which is a direct reflection of a company's culture.

WEAK ORGANIZATIONAL CULTURE

One thing that the most successful companies share is a strong culture. I like to think of an organization's culture as the commonly accepted beliefs, values, and emotional environment that exist in the workplace. More and more organizations are measuring the health of their culture by assessing team member engagement. Boston University professor William Kahn identified employee engagement as the level of emotional investment they have in what they do. Engaged team members are involved, productive, and understand they are working toward both their own goals *and* the goals of the company. This sense of purpose is critical to maintaining a positive emotional environment. Team members who understand how they fit into the big picture know they have a larger reason to work beyond simply earning a paycheck.

This means that if you want engaged workers, you have to understand each team member's goals, and make it known what the goals of the organization are. When common goals don't exist, each individual creates their own agenda and many times this isn't supportive of the organization. It also has to be understood that you, as the leader and representative of the organization, are genuinely interested in the opinions and voices of the team. All humans want to feel heard, valued, and appreciated for their time and talent. This small but critical gesture develops trust throughout all levels of the organization and helps cultivate problem-solvers who aren't afraid to speak up if they think they can improve the status quo.

If you want engaged workers, you have to understand each team member's goals, and make it known what the goals of the organization are.

So, What's The Problem?

In his 1990 study about employee engagement, William Kahn describes the ability of an employee to be their "full self" at work without fear of negative impact to their self-image, status, or career as "psychological safety".[5] I'll discuss this in greater detail later, but the important thing to take from this for now is that psychological safety can be significantly improved through clear and frequent communication between organizational leaders and their staff. Notice I said *between* the leaders and staff. This means there has to be open, two-way communication—not just from the top down. Doing this will support a sense of belonging and strengthen relationships.

This enhancement of the relationship between managers and staff, the feeling of psychological safety, and the engagement of team members is exactly what forms a strong culture and creates an environment that people don't want to leave. Based on the information in the previous section about the cost of employee turnover, building a strong culture should be a very high priority. It should also be fairly obvious now that the same general problem is threaded between high turnover and a weak culture—poor communication.

POOR COMMUNICATION

One of the biggest challenges most leaders face has to do with communication. Monthly meetings, town halls, and quarterly evaluations may be fueled by the intention to help teams communicate, but the impact is usually the opposite. In the salon industry, as I'm sure is the case in other smaller organizations, most leaders have learned to communicate from the leaders who came ahead of them. That can be a good thing if they followed great leaders with strong communication skills. But if they are emulating weak examples, they are most likely poor communicators running ineffective meetings. It's not a surprise that so many business owners and team leaders abandon regular meetings, thinking that the meetings are the problem instead of working on more effective communication.

I totally understand how easy it is to keep pushing communication skills to the bottom of the priority list. It's such a broad topic and can feel overwhelming, so a lot of times we simply avoid it altogether, hoping the team figures it out on its own. Avoidance is one of the brain's most powerful "safety mechanisms" where it believes it's protecting us, when in fact it's doing the opposite. Avoiding the problem almost never improves the situation. This is definitely the case when it comes to communication, because if it's not fixed it can lead to much larger problems that can ruin an organization.

Communication needs to be broken down into systems, but most leaders don't know which systems are the most effective at strengthening the team and have never had the training to figure it out. Leaders try to run some form of regular meetings, whether it be daily, weekly, or monthly, but because they don't fully understand the intricate details that make these meetings productive, they give up on them. Or they continue to trudge through them, running meetings that result in the opposite of what they needed out of them. So why do so many potentially good leaders run such terrible meetings?

Avoiding the problem almost never improves the situation—especially when dealing with communication.

EDUCATION HAS FAILED US

Let's take a trip down memory lane. Think about learning how to talk, when we were able to find our voice. Then about school where we learned more complex words, as well as how to write and read them. We learned punctuation and grammar and even some words we shouldn't say. But the thing we did not learn is what happens in our bodies when we exchange words with others. We did not learn about the chemicals that are released that either open us up to trusting, sharing, and bonding, or shut us down, causing us to withhold information and invoke behaviors that protect us. It may seem like I'm oversimplifying this, but our words either make people feel good or feel bad. They carry energy and are the bridge to building trust, or creating distrust, with each other.

Leaders don't usually fail at running effective daily meetings because they aren't good leaders. Honestly, it's not their fault—they've never been taught how to communicate effectively. It's so important for leaders to know how to use words to open team members up to new ideas, inspiration, motivation, and encouragement, helping them stay in the part of the brain that allows their best solutions to come through. This is what is possible when you have a good conversation—and an Intelligent Huddle™ is simply that, a conversation that you have with your team each day.

There is a lot of neuroscience that backs up what happens when we exchange words with another person. I'm going to share really simply why knowing this information will transform your conversations, interactions, and meetings with your team. I can say through experience in my own business, and from seeing results with so many of my clients, that you will see major changes take place when you apply this knowledge to your huddles, conversations, or any meeting with your team. Like anything else, it requires practice and consistency, which is the other reason daily huddles typically fail.

CONSISTENCY

I recently worked with a business owner named Sandy. She and her team set a goal to increase from $70,000 to $100,000 in sales per month, but they were not making progress. I asked if I could sit in on one of their huddles, and after watching the meeting, I could see the energy and the environment definitely needed some adjustments. They needed to generate new energy and get motivated and empowered to do more if they were going to hit their goal of $100,000. But this wasn't the biggest problem.

The blind spot revealed itself when I asked Sandy what time her huddles started each day. Sandy shared that the huddles did not happen daily because not enough of her team started at the same time. While we were looking at how she designed her team's schedule, she shared the frustration she felt and the stress it had caused the business. There were many days that clients requested service that could not be scheduled because team members had other needs and took those days off. Sandy was turning business away, losing revenue, and preventing her team from reaching their $100,000 goal.

I made it clear to Sandy that she had to determine the behaviors required for her team to meet the new goal and identify the current competing behaviors that were taking the team further from it. When she got honest with herself and saw how the schedule was impacting her business, she knew the best answer was to align the team member schedules and become consistent with daily huddles.

Sandy called a meeting for all team members and started by showing them how many requested appointments were being lost due to the current method of scheduling. Then, she highlighted that the goals of each stylist were directly affected by this lost revenue and showed how changing to a common start time would not only help the business, but would help everyone reach their personal goals as well. She also explained how utilizing huddles to come up with a daily game plan would improve team communication and remove barriers that were causing additional stress for everyone.

Of course, there was some initial pushback against what appeared to be "lost freedom" by the stylists. However, Sandy stayed firm in her decision, remained consistent with huddles and the new schedule, and kept her team focused on the bigger picture of how these changes would support the business, team, and each stylist. Sandy's team is now well on their way to reaching their goal. They have already achieved $90,000 per month after only four months and are on track to hit $100,000 by the end of the year.

So, What's The Problem?

The error Sandy made at first—one made by a lot of leaders—was that she set new goals with her team but didn't change the way she operated the business. Sandy realized that if she and her team wanted to reach their goal, she needed the huddles to happen at the same time every morning. She needed the consistency of daily huddles so she could communicate with her team and allow them to co-create solutions with her that benefited them and the business. By being part of the solution, the team felt a sense of purpose and accountability to put the business's needs first. Also, because the team met daily, they could see how the changes were impacting the business and that they were actually moving closer to their goal. They could also see that by focusing on a common, long-term goal instead of their short-term wants, they were now earning more money and achieving the financial freedom they desired. It was a win for all involved.

I am sharing this story with you because it was the consistency of the huddles that made Sandy's story successful. She needed to meet daily and communicate effectively with her team about the changes that needed to be made. The other thing Sandy did well was sharing the vision of how this process would improve all of their lives. As leaders, we have to help our team see how they can reach their goals while supporting the business. Not providing a clear vision for the team is another reason daily huddles fail.

As leaders, we have to help our team see how they can reach their goals while supporting the business.

LACK OF VISION

As humans we are wired to feel a sense of belonging. We want to find our tribes and contribute. If we don't know the vision for the day, month, or foreseeable future, we become disengaged and start to look for a place that can offer us this understanding.

One of the most common blind spots I find when I'm brought in to consult with a company is that they do not have a clear goal defined for their teams. Sometimes the only person that knows the numbers, benchmarks, or metrics that need to be hit to keep the business growing and healthy is the leader, or maybe the direct report under them. This is a huge problem for teams and one that will cause a lot of disengagement.

It is vitally important that all team members know how their role and responsibilities contribute to the overall success of the team. Additionally, knowing the benchmarks that they should track to see their progress will keep them engaged in their work. By tracking numbers each day, you will also see the victories you and your team should celebrate. This is another piece that makes the huddles valuable. Planning huddles with the agenda I share with you later in this book will ensure there is time to cover both the important numbers and celebrations. However, not using a proven agenda can often allow meetings get off track, lose focus, or waste time.

FOCUS AND EXCESSIVE TIME

Another big challenge I see a lot with morning huddles is keeping on topic, and on time. This becomes very discouraging and draining for both the leader and team. There must be an intention of how the meeting will run and a structure to deliver and receive important information. Daily huddles should be no more than fifteen minutes long. I actually shoot for twelve. Without a solid agenda and specific rules of engagement in place, it's very easy to lose control of both topics and time. While you want the huddle to be a place for open communication, you still need to guide the conversation. I've seen many cases where the leader loses control, team members begin to bring up topics the leader wasn't prepared for, and they start to shut down or react in a negative way.

Daily huddles need to be efficient and productive. They should be primed correctly to have people show up, stay on track, and have a way to co-create with everyone's ideas. Everybody should know where and how they will contribute. If this isn't established, leaders and teams start to see huddles as a waste of time. I will show you how easily this can be remedied later in the book, so don't worry!

Whatever you do, don't give up on daily meetings. I know it may seem like there are easier ways to communicate, but over the last five years consulting major businesses, I can assure you there are not.

LEAKING ENERGY YOU DON'T HAVE

Lack of clarity and poor communication are the primary reasons we leak energy. Yet it's interesting how many leaders think having a team meeting for twelve minutes a day is one of the problems. Most often, intentions are misunderstood due to lack of knowledge on how to communicate during huddles. Once daily meetings are seen as unproductive, leaders believe they aren't necessary and move to other tools to share information with their team. I've spoken with many business owners who say, "I don't need huddles, I just email my team on a regular basis." Or, "I prefer to use text messages, or an app like GroupMe." While these tools have their place, they are actually another primary cause of lost energy and can actually decrease clarity and communication within the team. Let me share with you some of the pitfalls to watch out for when choosing tools other than huddles.

Lack of clarity and poor communication are the primary reasons we leak energy.

Coordination Software and Apps

One resource I see leaders work with in place of daily huddles is the app called GroupMe. The general idea with this type of app is that your team is all part of a group that you can text at the same time. It's supposed to reduce time by allowing you to text once, instead of many times to each team member. Other tools like Microsoft Teams, Trello, Asana, and other coordination software systems serve a similar purpose, so the concepts I'm about to share will apply across the board.

All of these systems can serve a valuable purpose in an organization, but none of them can adequately replace an effective daily huddle. One thing that quickly increases my cortisol levels (the stress and arousal hormone) is being on a group chat first thing in the morning through my phone. I already have too many calls, text messages, and other emails coming through, so adding this as my primary way of communicating to my team is simply not a viable option.

One of the primary benefits of the daily huddle is it allows everyone on the team to feel a sense of belonging, which only comes from a back and forth conversation happening in person. Yes, there are resources available that help facilitate a more in-person feel, such as Zoom. But it takes a great facilitator to utilize these resources at the same level as doing meetings in person. While I think this is a good way to incorporate team members that are off location, I still don't believe it should be the primary method used. When everything takes place through technology, communication begins to feel very impersonal and loses effectiveness. Email and text messaging are great examples of this.

Emails and Texts

Communication over email or text is a totally different experience from conducting a real-time, back-and-forth conversation. So many important details and emotions get lost when everything happens through email. Having a conversation that is built on the harmony of push-and-pull energy, meaning a back-and-forth exchange of words, has a much higher impact.

Time is one resource we cannot get back, or get more of. When I first start working with a new client, they often tell me that meeting for fifteen minutes every day adds up to a lot of lost time. My challenge to them is, how often do they have to go back to their team to correct misunderstandings, clarify both intent and meaning of their message, or correct team members who think they understood but didn't really get it? How much time is wasted chasing down individuals who never actually opened your email? Or, how much energy is spent asking people if they got the email or the text message? When they really get honest with themselves and look at the time they spend outside of email reiterating the same messages, they start to understand why meeting in real time is so important. This is when some leaders say "No, emails work fine for me because I have an open-door policy. If there are questions, my team knows they can come in any time and talk with me." But this also presents challenges when considering leaking energy.

Open Door Policy

This policy blows my mind a little, knowing how the mind works. My first question to clients that utilize this tool is, "How productive are you when unpredictable distractions show up, often by people in a very emotionally-charged state, wanting to talk?" I think we both know the answer to this. Can you really be in your best mind after being triggered unexpectedly by a team member that probably hasn't thought through solutions before running into your office? My next question is, "Does everyone on your team show up and participate in your open-door policy, or is it the same people on your team over and over?" If team members see the same person, or the same few people, constantly in your office, it creates a psychological environment for them that feels less safe to express their concerns. If a team member doesn't feel safe to express themselves, they are less likely to remain engaged, further feeding turnover issues and a poor culture. Everyone has to have a safe avenue to share information with the leader that doesn't drain energy or have a negative impact on productivity.

I can tell you from leading a team for the past eleven years, when conflict or challenges happen, I want the information to be given to me in a space that both the team member(s) and I can safely take it in and process it. This is how I incorporate emails into the huddle system. I have an "open email policy."

I recommend creating a separate email account for the team to use that is your "open email" account and only use it for this purpose. When one of your team members has a challenge, or a great idea/solution, they can email the details. As the leader, you have to commit to checking it each morning, preferably before the daily huddle. When you are prepared in this manner, it will allow you to show up with your best energy to take in this type of information. Then, if the matter is appropriate for the entire team, you can bring it into the huddle and have the team co-create a solution for the challenge they are facing. If it is a conflict between coworkers, that should still be addressed in private with the team members involved.

A lot of challenges in the workplace are usually fairly simple, like housekeeping, or support systems that help achieve results, or simple disconnects between members with different roles that need to have a better understanding of how they support each other. These are all great areas to bring to the team to co-create solutions in a space where everyone expects this to happen. When there is a daily space to have a conversation with your team around this type of content, you will see more love come into the workspace, more trust being built, and people feeling like their voices are heard. Daily huddles help everyone understand how the work they do impacts the team and the business as a whole, not just themselves and their numbers.

DON'T WORRY – THERE IS HOPE!

I realize I have spent an entire chapter discussing problems within businesses and why it's common for leaders to fail at daily huddles, or at communication in general. What I really wanted to show you is that you are not alone. Businesses of all sizes and across industries struggle with team member turnover and poor culture. The critical takeaway from going deep into these problems is that communication is the root cause across the board. In fact, I wouldn't be surprised if I could trace 99% of all business problems back to communication.

The other key takeaway from this chapter is to realize that, despite the existence of a larger number of tools that could be used, having daily in-person team discussions with push-and-pull energy is the most effective way to fix issues, or to keep issues from forming. It may seem like other tools are easier, or take less time, but I promise doing the work to establish a solid daily huddle will pay back huge dividends. Holding conversations with your team and preparing a safe psychological environment where they feel heard and valued can have a tremendous impact on retention and building an amazing culture. But remember, the conversation has to be done the right way. There are many elements of neuroscience at play that are critical to the success of daily huddles—and this is where I can help.

Having daily in-person team discussions with push-and-pull energy is the most effective way to fix issues, or to keep issues from forming.

I am not a neuroscientist, but I am certified in **Conversational Intelligence®** **(C-IQ)**, which is a program:

> *"designed to enable corporate leaders and teams to elevate the quality of conversations and create positive change within their organization. Our programs are uniquely positioned to help leaders, and HR executives to influence the workplace culture, and the conversations that take place in an organization—bringing the organization to the next level of greatness."* [6]

I was tremendously blessed to learn directly from the late Judith E. Glaser, who created the concept and founded the program. Judith dedicated her life to understanding the neuroscience behind conversations. Her self-proclaimed purpose was to share how "words change your world" and how we could all create a much better world if we understood how to use words effectively. Inspiration from this training is just one unique element that I bring to daily huddles that nobody else is teaching—and why I call my system Intelligent Huddles™.

I have used this process with many clients across industries, from small businesses to Fortune 500 companies, and the results are always fantastic. I'm excited to share these concepts with you so you can incorporate them into your huddles as well. The next chapter will focus on explaining important elements of neuroscience (very simplified, don't panic) and how it incorporates into all conversations. Building on this knowledge, I will then provide the framework for implementing daily huddles in your organization.

Can you imagine if you showed up to work and something felt exciting at the beginning of every day? This is what an Intelligent Huddle™ will do for you and your team. In just twelve to fifteen minutes a day, your team can build a connection and a bond that will allow them to work through any challenges that come their way, become engaged team members, and enjoy a strong company culture that everyone can be proud of. So, what are you waiting for? Turn the page and discover the basics of neuroscience and elements of effective communication that you were never taught in school.

CHAPTER 2

Basics of Neuroscience

"Words have power, words are power, words could be your power also."

—**Mohammed Qatani**

Words are powerful. They activate energy and can literally change the chemical makeup in our bodies. How we choose to use words can cause people to lose trust, shut down, or isolate themselves from the team. Conversely, we can also use words to increase trust, creativity, innovation, connection, and help build a healthy culture. If words alone are this powerful, then we need to understand how to communicate with our team in a way that inspires them to be in their best mind.

Understanding some basic neuroscience quickly removes the mystery of why the words we say, especially as leaders, are so impactful. Different parts of the brain are responsible for specific roles, and certain chemicals can be regulated to enhance connection and trust during a conversation. Having this knowledge is like having a key that can unlock your team's true potential. It will improve your communication dramatically if you apply the knowledge properly, so let's start by discussing the different parts of the brain and their unique functions.

Words are powerful. They activate energy and can literally change the chemical makeup in our bodies.

THE SIX "BRAINS" OF COMMUNICATION

There are six different "brains" in our body that all contribute unique elements to communication—the primitive brain, the limbic system, the neocortex, the prefrontal cortex, the heart, and the gut. No, I haven't lost my mind. I realize that by the dictionary definition of *brain*, we only have one. But in order to understand some of the systems in our body that interpret signals and cause reactions, we

THE SIX "BRAINS" OF COMMUNICATION

3. NEOCORTEX
4. PREFRONTAL CORTEX
2. LIMBIC
1. PRIMITIVE BRAIN
5. HEART BRAIN
6. GUT BRAIN

Parts of the content presented here are adapted from Conversational Intelligence® and the work of Judith E. Glaser.

are going to categorize different parts of our brain and body for this discussion. Please understand that this breakdown is a greatly simplified explanation of how different regions of the brain contribute to communication. It is not intended to go much below the surface because deeper knowledge isn't necessary to understand how to communicate better. So with that disclaimer out of the way, let's start by taking a look at each of the different brains of communication.

The first brain we need to discuss is the primitive brain, which is made up of the cerebellum and brain stem. Neuroscientists believe this was the first part of the brain to develop in modern man and is the center for our basic instincts and survival. Also known as the reptilian brain, it controls breathing, heart rate, body temperature regulation, digestion, reproduction, and balance. Most of these functions happen without us "thinking" about them, as do other survival functions such as the "fight or flight" and "freeze or appease" responses. Basically, the primitive brain detects and responds to threats, creating chemical reactions in our body that give us the best chance to survive. The important thing to understand is that words also trigger parts of the primitive brain that signal safety or harm to those we are speaking to. If our communication seems familiar, calm, and confident, it will probably be perceived as safe. If it is unfamiliar, aggressive, or unsure, it may be perceived as a threat until proven otherwise. The primitive brain reacts first, helping you to survive long enough that a more advanced part of the brain, such as the limbic system, can help process what's actually going on.

The limbic system is the second level of processing within the brain. This section is made up of the hippocampus, amygdala, and the hypothalamus, and is located in the temporal lobe. The limbic system records a history of emotions created from situations that were either agreeable or disagreeable, then uses these memories to compare current situations with things you have experienced in the past to add another layer of understanding to communication. For instance, if a leader has a history of insulting a team member behind their back, and the team member knows this, it won't matter how calmly new communication is delivered from the leader, or how familiar the leader's tone may be. The limbic system of the team member will overrule the primitive brain and consider the situation threatening. **Conversational Intelligence®**, the result of years of work and research by Judith E. Glaser, explains that when the amygdala goes into overdrive a flood of negative emotional memories hijacks the limbic system. This "amygdala hijack" creates distrust and inhibits the ability to make new safety assessments. This can make it particularly difficult for a team to accept positive changes from a leader at first. The key to unlocking the hijacked limbic system and replacing negative memories with new, improved memories is to be consistent with non-threatening, trust-building communication. **C-IQ** recommends being conscious of the following elements while communicating with others:

Tone
Humiliation
Rejection
Exclusion
Anger
Territoriality
Status

Being aware of these THREATS during communication can help you avoid an amygdala hijack within your team, so they remain open to what you are saying and trust you as their leader.

The key to unlocking the hijacked limbic system and replacing negative memories with new, improved memories is to be consistent with non-threatening, trust-building communication.

Another function of the limbic system is to decipher the social context of a situation. For example, if a fire alarm goes off and you initially panic a little, your limbic system will determine the level of panic shown by others around you, to influence your decision to run or remain calm. It also deciphers where you fit within the social order, scans for inclusion or exclusion within the community, and nurtures and builds relationships and tribes. Team members need to feel safe to express their ideas and concerns without the fear of being excluded from the tribe or losing their position in the social order. Again, developing a consistent record of communication that creates positive emotions will supercharge your efforts to improve your team's psychological safety, trust, and ultimately, the organization's culture.

The third brain of communication is the neocortex, which is thought to be responsible for rational or objective thought. It is made up of several layers that cover the two hemispheres and technically contains four lobes—occipital, parietal, temporal, and frontal. These lobes are probably what most people think of when they picture a brain in their mind. See, you just used your neocortex to visualize the grooves and ridges that are commonly thought of as the brain. I discussed the temporal lobe already in the limbic system section, and will save the frontal lobe for the next section. So, for this part of the discussion, when I say "neocortex" I will mainly be talking about the occipital and parietal lobes.

Language, reasoning, sensory perception, and motor skills all originate in the neocortex. We are more conscious of things happening once they reach this part of the brain. This is where we start to *think* about what someone said, as opposed to simply reacting to it. The neocortex uses memories and emotions from the limbic system combined with what we see, hear, and feel, to process communication audibly, visually, and conceptually. The good news is, there isn't anything extra we need to do to appease the neocortex if we are being careful not to trigger the primitive brain or cause an amygdala hijack in the limbic system.

The fourth brain is the prefrontal cortex, or the frontal lobe. This part of the brain is sometimes referred to as the *executive* brain because it coordinates inputs from the other brains and the nervous system to integrate, heighten, or suppress the inputs as needed. It is responsible for our ability to envision the future, have empathy and compassion for others, make judgments in difficult situations, live in trust, and have integrity. When we communicate as leaders, it is important to help team members envision possibilities for themselves and the company, as well as co-create solutions to make those visions achievable.

Another key role that the prefrontal cortex plays is maintaining rational control over emotions. This ability is particularly important for a leader while communicating with their team. It's important to realize that just because we are leaders, it doesn't mean we don't have the same reactions from our primitive brain or limbic system that our team members may have. We can be triggered to react to threats like everyone else, so it's important to know that we can, and must, control our emotions in situations that may normally cause us to react poorly. Keeping in mind the THREATS acronym from earlier, recognizing when these triggers are occurring will be the first step to controlling emotion and redirecting the energy into something productive. That may be something as simple as allowing a team member to air a grievance in order to feel heard and valued, or something more complex that requires the co-creation of a solution by the entire team. Either way, the prefrontal cortex will play a major role.

Our fifth brain is the heart brain. The term "heart brain" was coined in 1991 by pioneer neuro-cardiologist Dr. J. Andrew Armour when he discovered the heart possessed a complex and intrinsic nervous system that is like a brain.[1] He expanded on the research done by

John and Beatrice Lacey that showed the heart actually communicates with the brain in ways that greatly affect how we perceive and react to the world around us. In fact, the heart communicates with the brain more than the brain communicates with the heart, according to the HeartMath Institute. Additionally, the heart is the largest generator of electromagnetic energy in our body; it creates a field of energy that extends out at least three feet in all directions. According to *Science of the Heart*, an overview of HeartMath Institute's research, "Evidence now supports the perspective that a subtle yet influential electromagnetic or 'energetic' communication system operates just below our conscious level of awareness."[2] The ability to sense what other people are feeling is an important factor in allowing us to communicate effectively with them. Our heart communicates signals that allow us to either sync with someone else, creating a bond, or oppose them, creating a foe. Next time you feel "magnetically drawn" to someone, know that you actually are.

> *The ability to sense what other people are feeling is an important factor in allowing us to communicate effectively with them.*

The sixth and final brain that impacts communication is the gut brain. The gut brain is primarily responsible for controlling digestion, but studies are showing now that there is more to this system than previously thought. Getting *butterflies* in your stomach when nervous, or having a *feeling in your gut* are not accidents. This is your gut brain communicating with your head brain, and it does so constantly. Research has shown that the majority of the communication from the gut to the brain happens via the vagus nerve.[3] This connection is called the gut-brain axis and is vital to normal life function.

One area of interest that is proving to impact many areas of health is the condition of the gut microbiome. Studies show that a lack of diversity in the gut microbiome can inhibit normal communication between the gut and brain, which increases levels of stress hormones in the body.[4] This is one of those "good to know" facts that can improve awareness about yourself and your team. People with increased stress hormones running through their systems are more easily triggered. You should also be aware of gut feelings you get as a leader about your team. There is an intelligence there that may not be fully understood, but it certainly should not be ignored. Plus, important neurochemicals are either created in the gut, or signaled by the gut that they need to be created.

NEUROCHEMICALS

Just as there are many different "brains" responsible for specific roles in the body, there are also different chemicals that are created to ensure these roles are carried out. Neurochemicals carry signals from nerve cells to target cells to regulate a multitude of functions throughout the body. While over one hundred different neurochemicals have been identified by scientists to date, there are only a couple that I need you to be intimately familiar with to improve communication—oxytocin and cortisol.

Oxytocin is the primary neurochemical that drives humans to be social creatures. It is created in the hypothalamus, then sent to the prefrontal cortex and other parts of the body as needed. Oxytocin is directly linked to reducing anxiety and increasing social confidence and loyalty.[5] Studies also show that oxytocin helps us understand what other people are thinking or feeling, which is proving to be more important than most realize.

Project Aristotle[6] was a massive internal study conducted by Google in 2012 that analyzed hundreds of teams to figure out why some succeeded and others didn't. Two teams could be made up of members that were nearly identical, yet one would succeed and one would fail. It didn't seem to matter if one team had a strong leader, a group of strong leaders, or if it was made up of complete introverts—there were no significant patterns among the members. So, they expanded their search to the team's behaviors. This is where the analysts started to note similarities among successful teams.

Two factors rose to the surface as vital to team success. First, successful teams allowed all members to speak equally. In fact, any time one person, or a small group of people, dominated the team's discussions, the collective intelligence declined. Second, teams that consistently experienced success had high "emotional intelligence," or EQ. Researchers such as John Mayer and Peter Salovey define EQ as "a person's ability to perceive, control, evaluate, and express emotions."[7] Teams that were made up of members who could identify emotions, evaluate how others felt, control their own emotions, and relate to others had an overall intelligence where the sum was greater than the individual parts. In other words, the successful teams had members that felt heard, valued, and appreciated for their time and talent— they felt psychologically safe as a team. Other elements did play an important role, such as clear goals and dependability, but Google's data indicated that, "psychological safety, more than anything else, was critical to making a team work."[8] The empathy that the high-performing teams expressed to create psychological safety would not have been possible without oxytocin.

Psychological safety, more than anything else, was critical to making a team work.

Another major benefit of getting oxytocin flowing within a team is that it helps strengthen trust, which is also essential to a high-performing organization. Paul J. Zak, a neuroscientist and author of the book *Trust Factor: The Science of Creating High-Performance Companies*, spent eight years measuring brain activity while people worked in order to uncover the aspects of culture that have the biggest impact on performance. He found that organizational trust was "a key part of culture that directly influences how willing your employees are to go above and beyond in their roles."[9] Further,

Zak conducted a nationally-representative survey of over a thousand working adults and found that employees working in high-trust companies:

- have 106% more energy at work
- are 76% more engaged at their jobs
- are 50% more productive
- suffer 40% less burnout
- are 50% more likely to stay with their employer over the next year
- and, 88% would recommend their company as a place to work to family and friends

Zak's findings were conclusive: "trust improves performance no matter how you measure it."[10] And when it comes to psychological safety, trust, and social bonding, oxytocin can be found at the root of it all.

"Trust improves performance no matter how you measure it."

—Paul J. Zak

Cortisol, on the other hand, is best known as a "stress hormone" as it is released during times of stress. It is made in the adrenal glands and provides vital changes to our system during a "fight or flight" situation. When we are in crisis, either perceived or real, cortisol is released and increases heart rate, blood pressure, blood glucose, respiration, and muscle tension as a response. It also limits systems that aren't critical to survival in the moment, such as digestion and reproduction.[11] And cortisol restricts communication across the vagus nerve, meaning wisdom from the gut and heart may no longer be reaching the brain.

Even though conversations are not typically "life or death" situations, even a small miscommunication can trigger a negative response that floods the body with cortisol. This causes people to close down to ideas and conversation, lose trust, and isolate themselves from others. Obviously, it's best if a cortisol response can be avoided altogether. Your first line of defense is steering clear of THREATS (tone, humiliation, rejection, exclusion, anger, territoriality, and status, as listed above) to the conversation. While *you* may be able to keep these elements in check, spotting them in others may indicate the conversation can't progress until the issue is resolved.

When I think about oxytocin and cortisol in relation to communication, I think of oxytocin as being represented by green (go), and cortisol as red (stop). If we want to move forward then we want more oxytocin flushing through the other person and ourselves. If the conversation is not going anywhere and we recognize that people are shutting down, or resisting others' ideas, then we are at a standstill because of cortisol. It is crucial to understand that our words are constantly giving others a green light to move with us in a conversation, or a red light to stop connecting with us and shut down. Once this concept is understood, it is easier to have awareness of what is actually happening during a conversation and purposely move it in a positive direction if it hits a red light.

> *It is crucial to understand that our words are constantly giving others a green light to move with us in a conversation, or a red light to stop connecting with us and shut down.*

The primitive brain is kind of like a dark, cold, lonely basement. It is the home of fear, stress, and survival. The executive part of our mind is like the balcony, where are view is clear. This is the region of the mind where creativity, solutions, and trust live. When having conversations with your team, or a team member, I always want to make sure I'm bringing people to the balcony, not sending them to the basement. Or, if needed, moving them from the basement to the balcony—from fear to clarity and trust. Essentially, you have to regulate neurochemical production to keep people operating in the best parts of their mind.

REGULATING OXYTOCIN AND CORTISOL

This is actually where the magic of **Conversational Intelligence®** happens. The foundation of neuroscience I've provided up to this point was all to help you understand what is happening in the brain and body during a conversation. Recognizing when someone is responding poorly during a conversation or meeting, and understanding the science behind why, will help you remain calm and be the leader they need you to be in that moment. The key is to down-regulate cortisol, and up-regulate oxytocin.

Down-regulation of cortisol happens by minimizing the types of conversation that cause fear, power plays, uncertainty, and the need to be right.[12] This means making sure you and other participants in the conversation are not excluding, judging, limiting, or criticizing others; dictating; or refusing to explore possibilities. Instead, reinforce the types of conversation that inspire transparency, relationship-building, understanding, a shared vision of success, truth, and empathy.[13] Up-regulating oxytocin can be done by ensuring you and other participants include everyone, show appreciation, remove limitations, celebrate wins, foster co-creation, and are open to discovering new possibilities.

Recognizing when someone is responding poorly during a conversation or meeting, and understanding the science behind why, will help you remain calm and be the leader they need you to be in that moment.

CHAPTER TAKEAWAYS

I hope after reading this chapter you can appreciate the true power of words. They don't just relay a message—they inspire an entire chain reaction within our bodies that can either build or destroy trust, psychological safety, and social bonds. Remember in the last chapter when I mentioned the Peakon study, *The Employee Voice*? Two of the top three answers from over 11 million employees said that better communication and a better relationship between leaders and team members would be the things they would change if they had a magic wand. Both of these elements can be achieved using the knowledge from this chapter.

Simply understanding that the primitive brain is where fear and survival originate, causing cortisol to course through our body, is empowering. When we recognize a negative response happening, we can purposefully up-regulate oxytocin and down-regulate cortisol by being aware of word choice and tone. It sounds simple, but this alone can move a person from the basement of their mind to the balcony, or prefrontal cortex. This type of awareness will dramatically improve both the communication and relationships within an organization. Understanding basic neuroscience also allows you to consciously create regular conversations with your team that are designed to release oxytocin, unlocking their most creative, trusting, and open potential. Studies like the one by Peakon are consistently showing similar results—employees who feel heard, valued, and appreciated for their time and talent are happy to stay with their current employer. These are the employees that feel psychologically safe, trust their organization, and spend time mostly in their executive brain.

Understanding the neuroscience behind good communication will help you in any conversation. Being able to change the state of a person from defensive, isolating, and fearful to collaborative, participating, and creative is literally a superpower that no leader should be without. We all have access to this superpower, but we have to develop it through consistent practice. When we do, we begin to build the kind of trust and relationship as a team that makes a great culture inevitable. The next chapter will discuss what I believe to be the best format for communicating with your team daily ... the huddle!

CHAPTER 3

Applying Neuroscience

"It's not what we do once in a while that shapes our lives. It's what we do consistently."
—**Anthony Robbins**

"Success is neither magical nor mysterious. Success is the natural consequence of consistently applying basic fundamentals."
—**Jim Rohn**

I love both of these quotes about consistency because they give such profound insight into where we are, and how we can get to where we want to be. We are consistent in our lives and our businesses, whether we are conscious of it or not. Tony Robbins suggests that we need to examine the areas where we are consistent to understand where we are and the circumstances that we currently face—good or bad. If you are unhappy with the current state of your business, what happens consistently to create that state? Are you avoiding tough conversations? Are you allowing drama where there should be teamwork? Are you communicating with your team so they can operate with clarity and purpose?

Don't feel bad if you've identified some areas for improvement. Nobody is running a perfect business. Some are more successful than others, but that is because they never get complacent with the status quo. Successful leaders are always looking for how to continuously improve. Your desire to improve your business doesn't mean you're doing something wrong, it means you care and want the best for your business and those that work with you.

Jim Rohn suggests that success is inevitable if we are consistent in applying basic fundamentals. I believe good communication is one of those fundamentals that Rohn is talking about. I spent the whole last chapter providing the neuroscience background required to be a consciously good communicator. However, knowing the information isn't enough. Applying that knowledge in individual conversations when the opportunity comes up isn't enough, either. Leaders need to apply these concepts every day in a consistent manner to truly see the amazing benefits they provide. That format *is* the daily huddle.

WHAT IS A DAILY HUDDLE?

Most of you have probably heard of the daily huddle (a.k.a. daily scrum, pow-wow, stand-up, etc.), or possibly even participated in them. Some reading this book, however, may be new to business or leadership, so let me provide a brief explanation of what a huddle means to me.

A huddle is a 10-15 minute meeting held at the start of each day that provides clarity about the specific goals for the day and how those goals apply to the vision for the company; reviews key performance indicators that inform the team about progress toward goals and vision; informs team members about important issues and company news; builds understanding of how each person contributes to company goals; highlights where daily obstacles may require extra support; provides a space for team members to co-create solutions to those obstacles, provide feedback, and be heard; and celebrates individual and company victories to boost and sustain energy and momentum. The daily huddle does not replace monthly, or quarterly meetings. Rather, it frees up time by dealing with the smaller items each day so the monthly or quarterly meetings can focus on larger concepts that need more in-depth discussion or time.

Ideally, huddles should be conducted in person so you can capitalize on both verbal and non-verbal cues to recognize how the team is showing up each day, mentally and emotionally. I realize many businesses have different start times for team members throughout the day, making this more challenging. My business is like this as well, so I'll address this concern later in the book. Ultimately, I see the huddle as a key component in building sustainable relationships with your team that creates a culture of loyalty, high performance, trust, innovation, togetherness, and LOVE.

> *Huddles should be conducted in person so you can capitalize on both verbal and non-verbal cues to recognize how the team is showing up each day, mentally and emotionally.*

Huddles are the best way a leader can have consistent communication with the whole team while bringing them to the best part of their minds at the start of each day. This is also the most effective way to pull the best vision and participation from team members. Listening to their ideas and co-creating solutions to their challenges builds trust and connection. All humans want to feel heard and valued as part of their basic needs of life. Huddles provide the opportunity to prime the work environment each day to infuse team members with oxytocin.

Unfortunately, there are plenty of stories about daily meetings that did not follow the principles outlined above. If you are skeptical about moving forward because you have not participated in effective huddles in the past, it's most likely because the person leading those meetings did not have the neuroscience background required to be effective. Destructive meetings are a possibility if the leader uses the meeting to regularly tear the team down. If you start each day with negativity, that is what will dominate throughout the day and it will kill productivity, trust, and loyalty. It is also very important to remember that a huddle is not a place where leaders do all the talking. I have been a part of meetings where the leader only uses it as a platform to "tell, sell, or yell" instead of supporting the team. Finally, a huddle is not the right place to address major challenges, or provide too much information, as that can become overwhelming for you and your team. Larger challenges may be identified during the huddle, then re-addressed at weekly or monthly meetings where more time is dedicated to solving them.

> *If you start each day with negativity, that is what will dominate throughout the day and it will kill productivity, trust, and loyalty.*

So, if you haven't had the best experiences with huddles in the past, please know the problem wasn't the meeting, it was the person running the meeting. It takes a strong leader with conscious communication skills to facilitate a short, but highly energized meeting that flows smoothly, generates engagement, and delivers information that adds value to the day. The fact that you are reading this book confirms that you are the exact type of leader needed to lead highly effective huddles and bring many benefits to your company and yourself.

BENEFITS OF THE DAILY HUDDLE

Up to this point I've spent a lot of time building a foundation around neuroscience and conscious communication. I have highlighted many research-proven benefits of building a psychologically safe space and fostering trust, such as lower turnover, higher productivity, and a strong culture. As I mentioned before, daily huddles are one of the easiest ways to consistently communicate with your team. They create a dependable routine and rhythm that team members will learn to count on to start each day. They pull creativity and innovation out of your team when they are the sharpest. And, they give leaders a chance to identify team members who may not be their "best self" early in the day, providing an opportunity to help shift their mood, inspire, or reinvigorate them in a positive way. No matter what industry you are in, daily huddles are key in bringing love, purpose, and a "people first" feeling into your environment. The following benefits are some that I've witnessed the most while consulting throughout different organizations.

Save Time

Almost every CEO or business leader that I've worked with starts out with the same major concern, "I already don't have time for the things on my plate, does this lady really think I can carve out 15 minutes every day to meet with my team?" Then they proceed to add up the minutes per week, multiply it by 52 weeks, then by the number of team members, and finally gasp at the total time "lost" by doing a daily huddle (It's 65 hours per team member, per year, by the way). Yes, if you do the math it looks like a lot of time, but what they are not counting is the time added back to their day because of the huddles.

Have you ever tallied up how long it takes you to write, proofread, and send out emails each day? How about how much time you take to read and respond to emails? Don't worry if you haven't, because I have some averages for you. According to *Harvard Business Review*, the average full-time worker in America spends a staggering 2.6 hours per day on emails.[1] Further, every time someone stops what they're doing to read an email, they lose focus on what they were working on. An article in the *Wall Street Journal* states that the average person needs twenty-three minutes to get fully back on task after an interruption.[2] I get it, not all emails are about topics that can be addressed in a huddle. But, if even *one* email a day can be avoided by addressing a topic, you could be saving yourself and your team significantly more time than 15 minutes each morning.

Huddles also provide a platform to ensure team members are all working to meet the goals for the day, week, and month. Individuals who may be unmotivated, or confused about their specific role, can slow their own productivity as well as anyone who has to take time to help them. It also creates a space to address challenges while they are still small. Solutions to minor concerns can often be co-created quickly if caught early. However, challenges that escalate can severely degrade the productivity of the team and take much more time to deal with.

So, when business leaders ask if I really expect them to find time every day, my answer is always, "YES! I know there are 15 minutes available to have effective, daily, face-to-face communication with your team." Huddles will save you time, despite what the simple math indicates.

Huddles will save you time, despite what the simple math indicates.

Reduce Stress

I realized that my husband and I would share small parts of our goals for our company in our monthly meetings, but we never provided the whole vision so our team members could get fully behind us. We were the only ones that knew what needed to happen each day to make our business as successful as it could be. We would also say things almost daily such as, "We need to make sure and let the team know _____." Or, "We need to talk to the team about _____." But these issues that seemed important in the moment never went anywhere. Eventually, we felt overwhelmed and these things would end up dominating our monthly meetings. Because we had so many little things to address, we only had time for "tell and sell" meetings that were full of comments like, "We need to make sure we are doing this" or, "We need to stop leaving that behind." Again, all talk with no real plan for action. Our "follow-up" would be us getting home from a long day of work and trying to send out emails. This was the only time we had to share victories with team members to try to keep them motivated and acknowledged. It felt like there was never enough time in the day.

This is when I realized how much more productive we would be as leaders and as a team if we had daily huddles to stay on top of the little things that make the big things possible. I felt relief from some of the pressure and overwhelm almost instantly after starting daily huddles. It felt like everyone that was included in making the team successful was being brought together to understand how their actions, behaviors, and energy was affecting and impacting our day. And huddles became my opportunity to apply the neuroscience that I knew was critical to achieving the highest potential possible.

Create A Team of Problem-Solvers

The responsibility of being the leader can sometimes create pressure to have all the answers. This is especially true as business owners or high-level leaders who have been in the company for a long time. We try to do it all, usually leaving time to accomplish nothing.

The best leaders, however, know they don't have all the answers. Instead of trying to do it all, they understand that their team is a resource that can often provide new perspectives and provide solutions they wouldn't have come up with on their own. Using huddles to up-regulate oxytocin and move team members to the executive part of their brain brings out their best ideas and innovation. In addition, consistently addressing small issues in huddles sharpens the team's problem-solving skills and demonstrates that it's safe to provide input. This creates a team you can count on, one that is capable of solving challenges quickly and working toward one vision. Teams like this develop into partnerships, formed on a foundation of trust and bonding that is key to keeping good people in the organization.

Align Goals and Increase Productivity

As a leader, you have a responsibility to find a way to align the goals of the company and the dreams of your team members if feasible. Huddles create a space for you to listen to the aspirations of your team and share the company's goals with them. Making this effort provides clarity about how team members are contributing to the company, while moving closer to their goals and dreams at the same time. This understanding creates a larger sense of purpose at work instead of simply working to earn a living.

The leaders of a company have goals and dreams about how they want the company to grow. And each member of the organization has personal goals and dreams. All too often, business owners treat revenue goals, or any other number-oriented goal, as a reactive process: at the end of each month somebody looks at the numbers and decides if the team did or did not meet expectations. Then they react. Usually by telling team members they need to work harder, or faster, to achieve the goal the next month. They are always chasing the numbers instead of being proactive by addressing the numbers each day in a huddle.

You may feel like some company goals, especially ones based in revenue, are not "need to know" information for your team members. They are supposed to come to work, do a good job, and be happy they have a paycheck, right? Not at all. A sense of belonging to a tribe and contributing to a cause are elements that are vital for humans to feel a sense of fulfillment in their lives. Whether they are consciously aware of it or not, each person needs to know that what they are doing is contributing to something bigger. By reviewing the numbers with your team daily, you get to show everyone how they impact the team and the company each time they either achieve or don't achieve their own goals. Knowing their numbers are going to be reviewed every day also invokes a sense of personal accountability to the rest of the team. This commitment to the tribe inspires more responsible choices throughout the day, which improves chances even more of accomplishing daily goals.

A sense of belonging to a tribe and contributing to a cause are elements that are vital for humans to feel a sense of fulfillment in their lives.

But Drea, won't this just embarrass people if you call them out for not reaching their goals? It won't necessarily be comfortable for them, but the purpose for bringing this up daily is so other team members, and you as the leader, can rally around the person and show support in helping them make their goals. When they see that they aren't going to be punished, or humiliated, and instead experience caring support, they begin to feel psychologically safe and their performance is sure to improve. This also improves trust and the overall feeling of belonging within an organization, which is when an employee is most productive.

Daily huddles allow you to work with your team to co-create a plan to reach individual and team goals. If you want numbers to grow, then it's important that everyone be accountable for their role in the team's success. Huddles also provide a time for daily celebration when goals are met, charging team members with new energy and motivation. They also allow for small course corrections that can help the team recover before the goal is out of reach. The numbers of the business tell a story, but the story can only be fully understood if it is told every day. It may be uncomfortable at first, but reviewing the numbers daily will allow you to become proactive instead of reactive. And, it will help team members stay on track and find purpose by aligning their personal goals with those of the company.

Improve Team Adaptability

Change is the one thing that is always constant in everyone's life. When a team can successfully adapt to constantly changing circumstances, they are almost guaranteed to succeed. Huddles provide a way to move through changes with ease, instead of resistance. Just like reacting to numbers, if you are only meeting with your team once a week, or worse, once a month, you may be reacting to changes as well. Reacting to changes makes leadership much harder because it always feels like you are trying to catch up. The daily ritual of huddles allows the team to talk about what changes they are currently moving through, and what may be on the horizon. This daily discussion allows you to work with your team and have plans in place that have been thought through and communicated, so adapting to change doesn't seem so dramatic. Of course, not all changes will be predictable, but having a rhythm of meeting and discussing possibilities creates a more adaptable group.

CHAPTER TAKEAWAYS

Daily huddles get your team talking every day. Why wouldn't you want your team discussing valuable information and topics that support the success of the team and the business? Anything that needs attention gets addressed, solved, or celebrated in real time. Huddles allow you to quickly get everyone on the same page so that daily tasks become less overwhelming and actually get completed. It's the small steps taken every day that lead to the big finish, or in the words of Jim Rohn, "Success is the natural consequence of consistently applying basic fundamentals."

When a huddle is executed using my method, you will see an increase in productivity, revenue, team engagement, organizational trust, and the strength of the culture. You will notice a decrease in time needed to communicate to your team, less stress about daily tasks, and less employee turnover (which means less time spent training new team members). Your team will be more involved with the business and become accountable for meeting personal and company goals. And, having a system like Intelligent Huddles™ shows that you are putting people first and making the team members a priority. I hope by now you can see how beneficial huddles can be for your company and any resistance you may have had has faded away.

When I am brought in to work with a company that wants to make changes and the leader doesn't meet with their team regularly, I can tell they know they should, but feel overwhelmed by the idea of having to get the team on board, adjust the daily schedule, and work to make huddles possible. Feeling overwhelmed at this point is **totally normal**. Success cannot come, or be sustained, without the systems, rituals, and tools in place to allow it to happen. I understand there is a little work that needs to be done up front, but it really isn't that hard and the return on investment will pay you back as long as you continue to do huddles.

> *Success cannot come, or be sustained, without the systems, rituals, and tools in place to allow it to happen.*

Look, you would not be reading this book if your days were running smoothly and your team was clear on the daily vision. It's not your fault. I'm guessing nobody ever taught you the correct way to run a huddle, or the benefits they might provide. Furthermore, there's even less chance somebody addressed the neuroscience behind good communication. So, congratulations! You are in the right place. The rest of this book will provide my step-by-step action plan to implement daily huddles in your business … the intelligent way!

CHAPTER 4

It Starts With You

The world is changed by your example, not your opinion.

—**Paulo Coelho**

I know you must be excited to jump right in and start your huddles tomorrow. But, before you "launch" your daily huddle program, there are some critical elements you should have in place to ensure success. As the quote by Paulo Coelho above implies, the success of your huddle program starts with you—the leader. The team members of your organization will never have more energy or excitement for something than you. This is why it's critical to consistently display the proper mindset, demonstrate the discipline and commitment necessary, and have a plan thoroughly mapped out. Once daily huddles are running, you should be prepared to provide support in areas your team identifies as obstacles each day. You will need to follow up on progress, or be ready to co-create a recovery plan to get back on track if commitments or goals aren't being met. You should also be ready to celebrate and aspire as a group, as this is what will keep you and your team inspired and allow it to reach its highest potential.

> *The team members of your organization will never have more energy or excitement for something than you.*

I realize you may feel a little overwhelmed and this is totally normal! Change always seems daunting at first. However, you have an advantage over most leaders. I am providing years of training, experience, case studies, and expertise in this book so you have all the tools you need to succeed. Some of the steps I discuss may sound like common sense, however, it's the common practice that is usually missing. This is actually a process that will not only grow your team in many ways, but will also grow your skills as a leader.

I want you to have the best foundation possible to find success through huddles, so the first area I will address in this chapter is mindset. Mindset is the most important foundational element, so it is discussed in depth.

As the leader, you will need to be mentally and emotionally prepared for pushback from your team, able to manage your emotions during huddle conversations, and able to self-regulate your own oxytocin and cortisol responses. This isn't as hard as it might sound, and the mindset adjustments presented will not only improve your effectiveness while working, but will benefit your personal time and relationships as well.

Next, I will express the importance of having a reliable support network. There will be times when you are either unable to lead the huddle, or wish to give a team member an opportunity to grow as a leader. During these times you will want a reliable group of delegates who are trained and ready to lead.

The final element you will need to prepare yourself is to get clear on your own aspirations for the company. Being able to define what you and the team are working towards is needed for unity, vision, and purpose. All of these are elements you, as the leader, will need to have clarity on before starting a huddle program. They will prepare you and the team for maximum efficiency and effectiveness to see results faster. So, let's start by exploring the mindset of the leader and how this can improve so many areas of your work and personal life.

MINDSET

Success with huddles comes through consistency, but this can only happen if the leader is consistent. Do you currently show up at the same time, on time, every day? Do you regularly provide positive feedback to your team members? Do you have the routine in your life that you are going to be asking other team members to commit to? Are you taking care of your own basic needs? These are some of the questions to think through before starting your huddle program. If the answer to any of these questions is no, then you must start by aligning your behaviors with the necessary values and beliefs to be successful.

> *Success with huddles comes through consistency, but this can only happen if the leader is consistent.*

Developing the right mindset is the most important step to bringing meaningful, valuable huddles into your team's culture. Change is never easy, so even though starting a huddle program is a series of simple steps, the brain will try to make them appear more difficult because we are wired to fear change. You have to be mentally strong to be a leader and you have to be committed to staying strong as you create change for your team members.

One challenge that causes a great deal of stress among many of the leaders I have worked with is knowing that changes are required in the team in order to see changes in the business, but not wanting those changes to affect their personal lives. This is rarely possible, as it is a person's mindset that drives their actions, both in their personal life and while at work. Most people would rather hold on to their comfortable routines and schedules that they think bring them freedom. But, what if the opposite were true? What if the very routines that keep you comfortable are the things that keep you from achieving your highest dreams? As a leader, this is a question you must ask yourself. Huddles will be a change in the environment and you may receive pushback from the team. You will certainly suffer some setbacks in the program, but you must remain committed, ready to lean in to change and in to what may feel like sacrifices so you can achieve greater success as a team. You will need to develop a level of mental toughness to succeed and display consistently that you are 100% committed to huddles. Without this mindset, you will have a much harder road to travel to reach the success you want.

In order to understand ... and change ... our mindset, we first need to become aware of our patterns of thinking. There is a level of self-awareness required to understand our personal mental model and the beliefs that hinder us. These are the elements that create our personal reality, so without self-awareness we cannot create change. Without self-awareness, we default to behaviors that continue to limit our ability to create what we want in our lives. We live more on the reactive side and have very little control over our impulses. Developing and raising self-awareness gives us the ability to respond and think through whatever we are facing and lean into our guiding values to make the best choices.

According to Daniel Golemen, author of *Emotional Intelligence*, "Self-awareness is defined as the ability to recognize your emotions as well as how they affect your performance and your interactions with others." This is especially important in huddles because it allows us to recognize when our emotions are triggered. It alerts us when a cortisol response happens that puts us into our primitive mind instead of our executive brain. In turn, this awareness allows us to have measured, productive conversations, even when things seem like they could go down an unproductive path.

> *What if the very routines that keep you comfortable are the things that keep you from achieving your highest dreams?*

Developing self-awareness is a continual practice that can be strengthened through mindfulness exercises. Research shows that leaders who make a daily practice of mindfulness exercises increase their ability to focus, stay calmer under stress, have better memory, and have increased empathy. Some of the most common exercises are meditation, breathing exercises, and journaling. I have a ritual of meditating and breathing every morning. If I notice any uneasy feeling or something ruminating during these exercises, then I journal about it in a notebook, or even on the "Notes" app on my phone, just to get out whatever is ruminating. A lot of times, it's something as simple as an overwhelming to-do list, which is common to many leaders. Not knowing how I'm going to fit everything in can be a very big energy drain and take me out of a good mindset. Being able to revisit my list, put some deadlines by the items, and even add some things to it, allows me to get centered and to step back into being present. Showing up each day to lead without this excess baggage is very important and allows me to bring my best state of mind to each huddle. You can download my guide of top mindfulness exercises for yourself and your team at www.dreahemmer.com/huddleresources.

Developing your own mindfulness practice that can enhance or develop self-awareness is extremely important. You have to become aware of how you're showing up every day and the energy you are bringing to the huddle since your team will be taking their cue from you. While breathing exercises, meditation, and journaling are amazing self-awareness tools, there are often life-events outside of work that require more than what these tools offer. It is during these times that we may need to lean on other leaders on the team. So the next element to have in place before starting a huddle program is knowing who your support network will be.

> *Become aware of how you're showing up every day and the energy you are bringing to the huddle since your team will be taking their cue from you.*

YOU WILL NEED SUPPORT

I was recently on a call with one of my business coaching clients and even through my computer, I could see that her energy was very low. She was visibly tired, disorganized, and overwhelmed. Even the color of her skin showed she was not in a good place. All of her verbal and nonverbal cues, or interaction dynamics, demonstrated how emotionally stuck she was. I started our session by asking what she wanted to get out of our time together, and she said, "I think I just need to talk about my personal life." It turned out she was going through a terrible breakup and it was dominating her thoughts and energy. I made it very clear that I was empathetic, and listened as she told her story, but as her business coach, it was also my obligation to make her aware of the impact this was having on her business.

After asking some detailed questions about how her business was going, it was very apparent nobody was providing direction to her team. Nobody was influencing them to greatness. She was basically avoiding going into work, hoping her team would simply do what they needed to do. The person they looked to for daily guidance was absent, and the business was feeling the negative consequences of her absence. If my client would have had a different mindset about the importance of her morning huddles, she could have had someone else designated to pick up the leadership role while she was incapable of leading. She didn't develop her support network early, so a challenge in her personal life snowballed into business challenges as well.

When my dad passed away, I could not be emotionally present for my team. I was so beside myself I couldn't even figure out where I was at, let alone lead a team where they needed to go. Luckily, I knew when I started my program that I wouldn't be able to lead every huddle. Obstacles are an unavoidable part of life, so I trained other team members to run the huddles as well. Not only did this take some of the pressure off of me, but it gave team members the opportunity to grow and develop their own leadership abilities. Having a support network in place during this time allowed my business to continue without skipping a beat. Plus, I was able to take the time I needed to heal without worrying about my team.

You will want to give some thought to who you choose to be your support. There needs to be at least one other person who can confidently lead huddles in your absence. Ideally, there will be 2-3 leaders that have been in the organization for some time that you groom for this position. You may already know who on your team is demonstrating strong leadership qualities and is naturally rising to the top. If so, great! If not, then here are a few questions to ask yourself when evaluating who to bring into the support network:

- Who do you trust when you leave?
- Who fulfills commitments?
- Who has energy and is excited about life?
- Who shows up on time?
- Who exemplifies the culture you desire?
- Who regularly supports others without being asked?

- Who do the team members trust and respect?
- Who consistently influences the team in a positive way?

While this list of questions may not be exhaustive, it should start to give you an idea of the type of person that will do well leading huddles. Even though it may seem like an easy solution, I do not recommend rotating through everyone on the team just to "keep it fair." This devalues the position and removes the feeling of responsibility and pride that developing leaders should feel. Also, the most senior member of the team does not necessarily equal the most qualified for the job. Total time served can be a consideration, but should not be the deciding factor. Think through the above questions and pick the best person/people for the job. Remember, this is all being put in action to improve the company and achieve the team's highest potential—potential that must be realized to achieve the company's highest aspirations.

GETTING CLEAR ON COMPANY GOALS AND ASPIRATIONS

Team members cannot work toward company goals if they don't know or understand what they are. This may seem like an obvious statement, but you would be surprised how many times I work with leaders who have not shared company goals with team members. This creates lots of frustration for both the team and the leader, as goals are regularly missed. As I stated in the last chapter, a sense of belonging to a tribe and contributing to a cause are elements that are vital for humans to feel a sense of fulfillment in their lives. Whether they are consciously aware of it or not, each person needs to know that what they are doing is contributing to something bigger. Furthermore, team members will find even greater purpose and have stronger drive to achieve company goals if they are in some way aligned with their own aspirations.

I define goals as measurable milestones that lead to a bigger dream, or aspiration. As an example, you may aspire to run the top salon, dental clinic, or accounting firm in your city. Goals that must be reached to achieve this dream may include a specific amount of revenue, or a total number of clients served in a year. Breaking these annual goals down into monthly, weekly, and even daily goals will provide quantifiable numbers that help you determine if you are on track. So before starting a huddle program, you need to identify and define very clear aspirations and goals that you will share with the team and track during each huddle.

I'm guessing most reading this book will have some aspirations already identified. Other aspirations may be revealed by thinking about why you want to implement daily huddles. If anything was possible, what would you go for? Where can your team or existing systems improve? What parts of your business are merely existing when they could be thriving? What elements of the business keep it sustainable that you want to strengthen? As you think through the answers to these questions, more aspirations and subsequent goals will start to become clear on their own.

Team members cannot work toward company goals if they don't know or understand what they are.

Once you have determined your aspirations and goals, your vision will be clear. All you have to do is identify the best metrics for tracking your progress. These are known as Key Performance Indicators (KPIs) and may be different from business to business. I have listed just a few of the most common KPIs below to give an example:

Revenue: This is probably the most common number tracked by businesses. It is a raw number that indicates overall performance, but should be compared against other KPIs to give an honest account of the health of the business.

Customer Lifetime Value (CLV): This KPI shows you the value of a long-term relationship with a customer and may reveal how long you must retain a customer before generating a profit.

Customer Acquisition Cost (CAC): Knowing how much it costs in advertising and other expenses to get a new customer in the door helps determine the service or product price required to be profitable.

Customer Satisfaction & Retention: This KPI is fairly self-explanatory, but is important to calculate potential recurring revenue and the impact that customer lifetime value may have on your business.

Number of Customers: By determining the number of customers you have served over a period of time you can calculate growth and determine other needs, such as when to add more team members or expand your business.

Employee Turnover Rate (ETR): This KPI is a direct indicator of workplace culture, environment, and company trust. A high ETR can be a major drain on revenue if you constantly have to find, hire, and train new team members.

Employee Satisfaction: Determining the happiness of your team members should indicate trends as to whether or not the culture of the company is improving, trust is building, or the environment needs to change. Determining this KPI through surveys and other forms of feedback may indicate the direction of ETR before it actually changes.

Again, this is a very short list of possible KPIs that can be tracked. One of the most complete lists I have seen can be found here: https://www.scoro.com/blog/key-performance-indicators-examples. This blog post provides a list of 136 KPIs, which should allow you to find just about any tracking metric you may need.

You will want to keep the number of KPIs reasonable, so narrow the list down to the most appropriate metrics for your goal. One or two KPIs per goal should be adequate. Finally, make sure each KPI is well-defined and quantifiable, crucial to achieving your goal, and communicated clearly to all team members. With vision defined, goals set, and KPIs determined to track progress, your next task will be to align company aspirations with those of the team members.

> *Make sure each KPI is well-defined and quantifiable, crucial to achieving your goal, and communicated clearly to all team members.*

Team members need to understand that huddles are not just about the company. They will benefit too, but you may need to explain how. Think, "What's In It For Them?" (WIIFT). Yes, being part of a tribe and working toward a bigger purpose within a company is important. But, to supercharge inspiration and motivation, team members must see how achieving goals for the company can also move them closer to their own aspirations.

ALIGNING WITH TEAM MEMBER ASPIRATIONS

In the past, I was afraid to hear the aspirations of my team members because I was concerned they wouldn't align with my vision for the company. This is what I call "ego-driven" leadership; I was totally stuck in "I" thinking and wanted everyone to agree with what I wanted. It didn't take long to realize how limiting this way of thinking was to my team members and my business. I witnessed firsthand how leading from an "I" and not a "we" mentality caused team member burnout. However, once we start to aspire as a team, then we can co-create a vision that benefits everyone.

Now I know that one of the most influential things I can do as a leader is to understand and support my team members in achieving their aspirations. When the aspirations of the company can be aligned with the aspirations of the team, then you will see motivation increase, participation rise, and culture grow.

There are a couple of ways to determine the aspirations of your team members. The first being to have individual meetings with each team member to learn about their dreams and develop a plan to support them, while they support the company. This is effective, but may also be a missed opportunity. When one contemplates their dreams, they move to the executive part of their brain, which is where creativity, trust, and problem-solving exist. Because of this, I recommend allowing team members to share aspirations during the daily huddles, the second option. Allow time in the first huddle to ask each team member what they would like to get out of the daily huddles. This will help co-create a team vision, eliminate pushback, and reinforce team buy-in.

When the aspirations of the company can be aligned with the aspirations of the team, then you will see motivation increase, participation rise, and culture grow.

When a leader understands how powerful aspirations are and can prepare a space where the team feels safe enough to share, it is a recipe for loyalty and trust, and motivates members to do their best work. As you learn more about the team and individual aspirations, you can find a way to align those desires with your own aspirations for the company, creating a truly symbiotic partnership.

CHAPTER TAKEAWAYS

The absolute most important element of preparing your huddle program is developing your own mindset as the leader. The discipline and commitment that you display will set the tone for your team to follow. Remember, as a general rule, your team will never have more energy about a project than you. Practicing daily mindfulness exercises can help bring greater self-awareness and ensure you approach each huddle with the best mindset. Don't forget to download the mindfulness exercises at www.dreahemmer.com/huddleresources.

While you should be the primary leader running the huddles, you should not be the only one capable of leading. Start training other team members who demonstrate leadership qualities early in the program so they can take over if you aren't available. The questions provided are a great place to start when choosing your support network, but don't be afraid to add details that are important to you and your organization.

The next element required to have defined prior to starting a daily huddle is the aspirations and goals of the company. You can never expect a team to work in unison toward a goal if they don't know what that goal is, or how it's tracked. Plan to briefly cover each goal and its KPIs each at every huddle so the team knows exactly where the company stands. Further, by aligning the personal aspirations with the company vision, you will create an environment that develops trust, loyalty, and motivated team members who are in a true partnership with you to succeed.

Just as this chapter covered the elements that you need to have detailed as the leader prior to starting a huddle program, the next chapter will cover external elements that are also critical to success. These are the final preparations needed before you can officially start your huddles.

CHAPTER 5

Final Preparation: Schedules, Space, & The Huddle Agenda

"Give me six hours to chop down a tree and I will spend the first four sharpening the axe."

—**Abraham Lincoln**

I hope it's obvious that everything in the book up to this point has been included to help you "sharpen your axe" and be prepared to run a successful huddle program. There are very few things as important to success as proper preparation. While success may not be guaranteed by the work you do up front, it will certainly provide a smoother road to travel.

The previous chapter was designed to get you, the leader, prepared for the challenge of leading daily huddles. This chapter is less about you and more about the external requirements that need to be in place prior to starting huddles that will help ensure your success. This chapter is broken into three areas that need to be in place prior to starting huddles: the schedule, priming the space, and creating an agenda. The first of these elements to have in place prior to starting your daily huddles is potentially the most sensitive, but must be acted upon to the maximum extent possible—aligning the team schedule.

SCHEDULE THE HUDDLE AND TEAM FOR SUCCESS

When you analyze the habits of highly successful people, the vast majority have one habit in common: they show up on time, at the same time, every morning. I have found this success habit to be just as important for huddles.

Huddles must be consistent and start at the same time every morning, so you will need to decide what time huddles will occur each day. I recommend analyzing a typical morning and scheduling the start time for 21 minutes before the majority of your team normally starts their day. You may even have to adjust schedules so the maximum number of team members can attend. This can be a scary thing for leaders who don't currently have a common start time for their team. This was the step that took the most courage for me to implement in my salon, but I knew I had to do it.

I also knew too many voices weighing in about the schedule could deter the whole program from happening, so I just had to be confident in my decision and let the team know a new change was coming that would strengthen them to go farther together. I did experience some pushback, as many leaders do, but once the team understood how this change would benefit them, the resistance disappeared and they began to embrace the process due to the results they were experiencing.

Huddles must be consistent and start at the same time every morning.

Final Preparation: Schedules, Space, & The Huddle Agenda

At first, you may have to persuade and advocate this new ritual to your team. They may be focused only on the short-term pain of changing their schedule, which is why you have to show them how this "sacrifice" can bring more joy, support, and financial freedom to their lives. You are going to have to trust yourself and the changes that need to happen for your huddles to be scheduled at the same time every day.

Even though many leaders are convinced that huddles are the answer they are looking for, they still use schedules as an excuse for why they can't do them. The most common excuse I hear when consulting is, "I don't think huddles could be possible for me and my team because everyone starts at different times in the morning." Another very common excuse is, "My team has a hard time showing up on time, so this would never work for them." I typically find that these leaders have gotten into the habit of either choosing not to pay attention to team member arrival times, or being afraid to enforce schedules for fear of losing team members. I try to shift the perspective for these leaders by explaining that you cannot meet team members' needs if the needs of the business are not being met first.

You cannot meet team members' needs if the needs of the business are not being met first.

I understand that moving from an ultra-flexible schedule to a consistent start time may seem like a hard or even unnecessary thing at first. However, this is the most valuable time for you to start each day with inspiration and motivation so your team can start *their* day off with purpose and positivity. Culture must be cultivated and fed in a healthy way each day to reach its full potential. Daily huddles that start at a consistent time are the fuel to ensure this happens. You *will* see positive changes in productivity, growth, and organizational trust, but consistency is key. Also, remember that the huddle is a dynamic interaction with your team. You will be constantly giving and receiving feedback, allowing you to co-create new actions as a team to make the huddles work for your unique situation. Variety will be important in your huddles to keep the time meaningful, so always be open to adjusting the ritual, but keep the start time consistent.

There are situations with smaller teams where it's not possible to bring more people in to participate in the huddles. Don't worry, huddles can be successful with as few as two people. That said, larger teams may have to break up into departments, or smaller groups. Consider this when you reach around twenty people, which is approximately the maximum size I have found to still be effective.

Finally, even if you adjust the schedule for maximum participation, there will still be times when team members cannot make it to the huddle in person. This is okay as resources are available to include participants virtually as well. This is a great way to include those team members that come in later in the day, or may be traveling. The key to making this work, once again, is proper preparation.

PREPARE THE SPACE

Preparing for the best environment to hold daily huddles is just as important as keeping a consistent start time each day. You have to prime the environment for both maximum participation and emotional safety. Maximum participation includes making sure the space is large enough to accommodate your entire team, even if they won't all be there every day. Plus, it means being prepared with technology to support team members who need to attend virtually.

If you have a private room that can be primed for maximum participation, then you are ahead of the game already. If not, you may have to get creative in where you host your huddles. I had to experiment a bit in my salon before settling on the best place for my team. We initially started on the salon floor, but we quickly

Final Preparation: Schedules, Space, & The Huddle Agenda

decided this allowed for too many distractions. My experience has shown that holding huddles in a space that is different from where the work takes place helps it feel special, and safer to the team.

Ideally, try to hold huddles in a place where team members can focus. It should be quiet, or as distraction free as possible. Lock the door if needed, or schedule the huddle to end before customers start showing up for the day. If able, choose an area with enough room for your team to form a close (but not uncomfortable) circle.

Finally, the space should be clean, organized, and supportive to the culture that you want to foster within your team. Even if you are forced to hold huddles in the same space where work happens, try to do something to set one area apart so everyone knows when they are gathered there, they are in the huddle space. You may be able to install a curtain divider to close off an area, or use a privacy screen divider to block off the view to distracting areas. Like I said before, you know your space and you may have to get a bit creative, but don't overlook the importance of setting the space apart and making it special. It will create a feeling of privacy, focus, and safety that will encourage participation.

Energy is best created when everyone is standing, preferably in a circle, where everyone feels equal.

Don't worry about adding chairs, tables, or additional furniture for comfort. The huddle is supposed to be quick and to the point. Energy is best created when everyone is standing, preferably in a circle, where everyone feels equal.

I also recommend keeping the technology to a minimum. Again, this minimizes distractions and the possibility of "glitches" disrupting the flow of your huddle. Keeping tools simple, like using a whiteboard to list agenda topics, will be easier than trying to create PowerPoint slides, or anything more formal. The only technology that is really required is the hardware that supports team members attending virtually.

The first item required to support virtual attendees is a phone, tablet, or a laptop with a camera. It would be ideal if this device was dedicated to huddles and not your personal phone, but this is optional. You certainly don't need random text messages or a call from your mom showing up on screen while you are discussing serious issues. If this is all you have, please make sure to activate the "Do Not Disturb" function on your device during each huddle. I recommend a phone or tablet because they can connect directly to various platforms needed to host the virtual huddles. That said, make sure you have a simple tripod, or place to secure your device. Shaky video is very distracting to the virtual participants and it's almost guaranteed that the person holding the camera will not be able to pay attention, or participate in the huddle. Also, if the area that you select for huddles is not well-lit, you may want to consider adding a cheap ring light, or LED shop light to help with video quality. Finally, make sure the camera is facing the team members. This gives a feeling of being part of the team and allows interaction with other team members. Do not focus solely on the leader of the huddles or it will feel like attendees are being talked to instead of having a team conversation.

The final element needed to support virtual attendees is a platform to host your meetings. Unfortunately, thanks to the pandemic many businesses are now very familiar with digital meeting platforms like Zoom and Microsoft Teams. If you are already using a platform that is reliable, then there's no reason to change. However, if you don't already have a platform to host your huddles, I would emphasize again keeping things simple. The primary aspects required are that the virtual room be private and that you be able to record the meeting. I personally like (and use) a private Facebook group specifically for this reason. Team members can be added to the group easily, they can participate with any mobile device, and most people are already familiar with Facebook so there is very little learning required. Also, after going live, the recording of the huddle is automatically stored in the group timeline so it can be watched later, accommodating team members who can't attend live. This is a very convenient feature that requires no additional interaction or time from the leader. Instagram TV or a private YouTube channel are also good options that have similar features.

Regardless of the equipment and platform that you choose, I highly recommend that you test the entire setup before your first huddle. This allows you to troubleshoot any problems in private, at your own pace, without the added pressure of the entire team staring at you while you try to fix a problem. Once everything is working correctly, you can shift your focus to preparing the last thing needed before officially beginning—the huddle agenda.

HUDDLE AGENDA

One of the most important parts of preparation is creating a flow for your huddle that takes advantage of the neuroscience you learned earlier in this book. Developing a well-thought-out agenda does this. When organized correctly, the huddle will move your team to the executive part of their brain first. This allows for productive conversation that pulls information, ideas, and solutions out of your team. It also primes your team to tackle their day with clarity and motivation. A good huddle agenda also gives you a way to keep the format and flow of information consistent each day, and makes sure you don't forget anything, which can be easy to do if the discussion goes off on a tangent. Basically, if you want your huddle program to be successful, you have to have an agenda that flows well and makes sense for your team. The purpose of this section is to walk you through some of the foundational elements that every agenda should include, as well as some optional elements that you can use to customize the agenda for your organization. The first element to discuss is making sure each huddle starts by moving team members into the executive part of their brain. This can be done one of two ways, either by celebrating victories or by asking discovery questions. I'll start with celebrating victories.

> *If you want your huddle program to be successful, you have to have an agenda that flows well and makes sense for your team.*

Celebrating Victories (2-3 minutes)

The first foundational element that should be in every huddle is celebration of victories. This element is critical for every team and should be the way each huddle begins. Many leaders understand the importance of celebrating with their team, but often don't create the time in an already busy schedule to do it. By starting each huddle with celebrations, the time is already built into the day and shows the team that you are putting a priority on acknowledging victories.

Celebrating the team, or team members, by acknowledging them for all types of victories creates oxytocin and dopamine. These chemicals naturally move people into the executive part of the brain and create a sense of value and belonging. Victories can be anything from major accomplishments by the company or team, to recognition of individual goals that have been met at work. As the leader, you will have to be up to speed on company, team, and individual goals so you are aware when achievements occur. However, meeting daily for huddles will bring awareness to these goals and allow you a simple way to track them as well.

If you are just getting started with huddles, identifying team victories may not be in your current habit pattern. Taking five minutes at the end of each day to reflect on the team performance will help establish this habit and keep you from trying to think of something right

Final Preparation: Schedules, Space, & The Huddle Agenda

before the huddle begins. Ask yourself, *Where were the day's victories? What is the story behind the numbers that made those victories possible? What did it take as a team to create the success in the day?* You want to ask yourself these questions and write down (that's important) the answers.

Of course, there may be times when the team is at the beginning of a project, or new goals have just been set, which makes it seem like there aren't any victories to celebrate yet. Worse yet, maybe your team is actually failing to meet their goals. Many leaders would choose not to celebrate in this situation, but please don't make this mistake! This is one time when it is the most important. When goals are not being met, it is a sign to the leader that the team needs better leadership, inspiration, or innovation. Support your team members by reframing their thinking around what they can do to change the current momentum. Have them brainstorm new actions that could support growth, or movement in the needed direction. Then, celebrate the brainstorming session or the best ideas that came out of it.

Many leaders understand the importance of celebrating with their team, but often don't create the time in an already busy schedule to do it.

There is always something positive that can be said to encourage the team. For instance, taking a moment to shine a light on behavior you wish to reinforce can be just as encouraging as acknowledging a personal win. Did you notice someone going out of their way to help another team member? Did you hear someone being extra courteous to a customer? Even asking team members what they are celebrating personally, outside of work, can be a great way to include celebration when other milestones haven't been met.

Another area to bring in celebration of victories is through discovery questions. Victories don't just have to be centered around numbers.

Victories can also be discovering something that wasn't known, or realizing a new aspiration. So, on the days where a specific victory around numbers may not be available, I like to ask discovery questions. Questions like, "If nothing was impossible, what would you accomplish today?" or "What are you the most inspired by when you think of our team?" or "What are you most grateful for at this moment?"

Questions like these are how you share and discover what is on your team members' hearts and minds. This is also how you open the space for trust at the beginning of your huddles and your team's day. As trust develops, the team will start to share both challenges and solutions they are thinking about. Download a list of 20 discovery questions that I personally use from my website, www.dreahemmer.com/huddleresources.

No matter what, you can always find a way to celebrate and acknowledge the small and big wins your team is having. The important aspect of celebrating victories in numbers or personal discoveries is to move the team into the most productive part of their brains.

KPI/Goal Review (2-3 minutes)

After celebrating goals that have been met, reviewing Key Performance Indicators (KPIs) that make sense for your team can help shape the priorities for the day and bring focus to team members who may need more clarity on where to put their energy. I *do not* endorse "chasing the numbers," or making KPIs the focus of these meetings. However, reviewing the numbers is necessary for a team to understand where they have been and where they are now, which brings clarity to where they need to go.

Consistent review of KPIs will also create a story that highlights where opportunities are hiding. Once they have been revealed, you can have a conversation with your team about how to co-create

Final Preparation: Schedules, Space, & The Huddle Agenda

solutions and capitalize on the opportunities being missed. This is why it's important to start each huddle with celebration or aspirations, to move the team into the executive part of their brains. Now, as the KPIs reveal a story that you'd like to edit, you can ask questions to draw out their best ideas, solutions, and creativity.

Consistent review of KPIs will create a story that highlights where opportunities are hiding.

For instance, if you wanted to grow a specific area of your business, you may ask the following questions: "When you think about growing the business in [the area where you see opportunity], what would we have to do differently as a team to make this happen? How could we spark creativity and actions to build new growth here?"

Asking questions with genuine curiosity, in a neutral and open-minded way, creates a space that encourages team members to participate. Can you imagine the trust you will generate when team members feel you believe in them enough to ask for their ideas? Plus, with new possibilities on the table, you can co-create an action plan as a team for how to accomplish the best outcome.

Asking questions with genuine curiosity, in a neutral and open-minded way, creates a space that encourages team members to participate.

Keep in mind, however, the huddle is primarily focused on what the team can do *today* to move toward the individual, team, and company goals. While huddles are great for discovering opportunities and bringing awareness to the team, there isn't a lot of time to solve complex problems. So if the KPI review reveals an opportunity that cannot be resolved within two to three minutes, you may have to schedule a meeting specifically for deeper discussions, or for co-creating a solution. At the very least, acknowledge the importance of the discussion and commit to revisiting the topic in the next huddle. Whether you are identifying KPIs that need more attention, or putting a new plan into action to capitalize on an opportunity, the next element of the agenda to keep good flow is discussing priorities, or projects for the day.

Priorities / Projects for the Day (3 minutes)

As I mentioned earlier, reviewing KPIs that make sense for your team can help shape the priorities for the day and bring focus to team members who may need more clarity on where to put their energy. This element doesn't have to take a lot of time, and shouldn't. The KPI review should highlight where priorities need to be placed. Then, it's simply a matter of verbalizing the priorities so everyone is clear on what they need to do. Or, in some organizations, team members may have to verbalize how they will prioritize their effort to accomplish specific goals. This can be pulled from your team by asking, "In 30 seconds or less, what is the most important thing for you to accomplish today to stay on track with the team goal?"

Similarly, there may be projects that need to be accomplished during the day to meet deadlines or satisfy other requirements. Asking members to share their project for the day creates a sense of accountability and responsibility to the team. It also helps others to understand the role each member plays in contributing to the team. This overall sense of belonging to a tribe and working towards a common goal also generates a willingness to help others if they are facing a challenge, which is the next element on the agenda.

Team Member Challenges (2 minutes)

At this point, everyone should have shared what they will focus on for the day. So, the next logical element for the agenda is identifying where team members feel they could face challenges. This may be one of the most important pieces of the huddle and can resolve many challenges before they occur.

Encourage team members to share tasks they feel anxious about, or barriers that could keep them from achieving their daily goal. This could be something simple, like getting a signature so they can keep moving forward. Or they may mention a part of their day where they will be very busy and could use support from others. Hearing where each team member may face challenges allows others to evaluate if they are able to provide support during those times. In fact, just sharing the challenge often sparks unexpected action from others and allows them to share ideas and solutions that otherwise might be missed. A good analogy to understand this concept is, if the colors red and blue always stayed apart, you would not know that the color purple was an option. Similarly, when team members don't share challenges with each other the best solutions may never be realized. However, when team members share possible solutions openly, the best ideas can be joined to form a solution that wouldn't exist otherwise.

> *Encourage team members to share tasks they feel anxious about, or barriers that could keep them from achieving their daily goal.*

A major key to success is that the team feels comfortable sharing where they may get stuck, which is one reason it is so important to establish a psychologically safe environment. One way to help ensure psychological safety is to build it into the rules of engagement (ROE is discussed fully in the next chapter). A simple rule that states, "Challenges must be followed by solutions, not opinions," goes a long way.

A great way to demonstrate psychological safety is to celebrate team members who share a challenge and anyone who offers solutions.

This positive reinforcement establishes that the huddle is a safe place to share concerns and receive support. Even if team members can only offer emotional support or encouragement, it strengthens the tribe mentality and builds trust and unity among the team.

Housekeeping / Announcements (1-2 minutes)

I don't consider housekeeping, or company announcements to be a foundational element, or required at every meeting. However, if you do have quick company announcements that the team needs to hear, then this can be a great way to get them out quickly and ensure the team has received the message. Emailing out the announcements later in the day means team members will still have to take time to read them, if they open the message at all. Letting announcements pile up for a weekly or monthly meeting can cause these engagements to be less productive and dreaded by team members.

While housekeeping — literally keeping the workplace neat and organized — may not be foundational for every huddle, it should not be overlooked. In fact, housekeeping is one of the most common concerns brought to leaders by team members. Studies have shown a decrease in motivation and creativity when a space is not kept tidy and clean. As the need arises, it is the huddle leader's responsibility to bring awareness to how everyone can contribute to leaving the work environment better than they found it, as well as encourage the team to take pride in their workspace. Rules of engagement can play a big role here and give a basis for measuring if the team is meeting the standards they set for themselves. Finally, if housekeeping continues to be an issue, then the huddle is the perfect place to have positive, solution-driven discussions on how to improve in this area.

Piece of Magic / Motivation / Inspiration (1-2 minutes)

The final element that should end every meeting is some sort of motivation, or inspiration. I call it a Piece of Magic during my huddles, but it's basically a way to make sure the team finishes the

Final Preparation: Schedules, Space, & The Huddle Agenda

huddle on a high note and starts their work day energized and feeling empowered. Here are three examples of how I finish each huddle with a piece of magic.

Power Words - Power words are words that encourage action by evoking emotion. The word "power" itself is a power word. I like to pick a word that generates a positive emotion or empowering feeling and make it the word of the day. I will pick something like, unstoppable, resilient, innovative, creative, efficient, potential, or any number of words that can inspire positive emotion. Then, I ask different team members to say what that word means to them and how they can apply it in their day. I also ask team members to think of a word that would describe their best energy, or to pick a word that describes how they will bring value to the team. Power words can be used in many ways, so don't be afraid to get creative!

Motivational Quotes – I love motivating, inspiring, and powerful quotes. Quotes are a great way to infuse a burst of motivation before starting a day. A well-chosen quote can create focus towards a specific goal or plan of action, or simply provide some wisdom for team members to try to apply to their tasks throughout the day. For instance, a quote by William James — "Act as if what you do makes a difference. It does" — inspires me to take pride in what I do, and remember that every team member is making a difference. Just Google "inspirational quotes" and you will have no shortage of content to choose from.

Positive Reviews – Service industries often live and die by the reviews they get. I find it extremely motivating to read the latest positive review to my team so they can feel the impact they are making. Hearing these types of responses from the customer can increase confidence in team members as well as provide gratification knowing they have done a good job.

Team members who start their day inspired and energized will be more productive and happier throughout the day. Whether you use one of these three techniques, or come up with a completely unique way to create your own piece of magic, I highly encourage you to find a way to end each huddle on a positive note.

If you would like an Intelligent Huddles™ agenda template that you can modify to fit your organization, you can download one from my website, www.dreahemmer.com/huddleresources. The elements listed above can be modified to best fit your organization. My advice, however, would be to make sure you include the foundational elements in some way or another. Also, you will want to keep the flow as shown on the agenda since it is designed to work with how the mind works. As you run a few daily huddles, you will begin to realize which elements need more (or less) time, which ones provide the best clarity and purpose for your team, and which types of magic are the most inspirational. In no time at all, you will be a master at running a productive, efficient huddle!

CHAPTER TAKEAWAYS

This was a very information-packed chapter, so don't feel bad if there's a little bit of overwhelm starting to creep in. Just take one section of this chapter at a time and the implementation will be totally doable. The most challenging part for many of the leaders I work with is making a schedule change for team members. Remember, this change is for the good of the company and the team. Here are the four steps for setting the huddle schedule:

1. Determine the best time at the beginning of the day/shift to schedule huddles.
2. Adjust team member schedules for maximum participation if necessary.
3. Plan for some team members to attend virtually.
4. Announce the new schedule to the team and stay consistent!

Additionally, making sure the space where you host the huddles supports your team and creates a safe, productive environment is

Final Preparation: Schedules, Space, & The Huddle Agenda

very important. Set up the space to be as private as possible, comfortable for the number of people that will attend, and accommodating for those who need to attend virtually.

Finally, creating an agenda that provides the proper flow and consistency for your huddles is paramount. Remember, one of the most important parts is getting team members in the proper mindset from the start, so ensure some sort of celebration is included at the beginning. Reviewing numbers, projects, and challenges for the day will bring clarity to where priorities and support should be focused. Then, finishing with some sort of piece of magic will help energize the team to go out and tackle the day.

Here is a quick breakdown of the agenda for easy reference:

1. **Celebrating Victories (2-3 minutes)**
2. **KPI/Goal Review (2-3 minutes)**
3. **Priorities / Projects for the Day (3 minutes)**
4. **Team Member Challenges (2 minutes)**
5. **Housekeeping / Announcements (1-2 minutes)**
6. **Piece of Magic / Motivation / Inspiration (1-2 minutes)**

Again, if you want to download resources like the list of discovery questions, or my Intelligent Huddles™ agenda template, you can get them from www.dreahemmer.com/huddleresources. Otherwise, jump right into the next chapter which will cover the art of running the huddle. I will address setting appropriate rules of engagement, ensuring proper conversational flow, and dealing with pushback, as these are all areas that can take your huddle from average to great.

CHAPTER 6

The Art of Running An Intelligent Huddle

Synergy does not mean giving up what we want. It means joining to co-create so each is able to receive even more of what attracts us through joining rather than opposing.

—**Barbara Marx Hubbard**

Congratulations! You've made it to the part where you can finally begin to implement your plan. So far, you've worked hard to understand the complexities of the mind by learning some basics of neuroscience. You've worked on your own mindfulness and awareness to prepare yourself to be a great huddle leader. You've prepared a physical space and aligned your team's schedules to maximize participation. Now you can bring the plan to your team and get their input in order to co-create the best huddle program for your organization.

The quote above, from Barbara Marx Hubbard, is perfect to lead off this chapter because the primary goal is to create synergy with your team through the daily huddle. There will be challenges, but by joining together daily you will be able to co-create solutions and make the huddle program even better than what you could possibly create on your own. Each section of this chapter supports creating synergy to bring both the organization and team members more of what is attractive to them.

The first section of this chapter discusses announcing the plan for daily huddles to your team. This can be a critical moment, as change typically creates an initial reaction of fear and resistance. I break down some of the biggest benefits to help show the team why there is so much to gain and little to fear. The next section explains the importance of setting huddle rules of engagement. This helps get the team co-creating right away and provides a structure that keeps the huddles consistent and orderly. Next, I will cover how to facilitate daily huddles with a conversational flow. This style of leading huddles creates an environment of inclusion and energizes creativity, which means everyone receives more from each gathering. Some team members may not get on board right away, but this can actually be a blessing in disguise. The last section provides guidance on how to recognize pushback and how to capitalize on it if it shows up.

There's no question that announcing something new to your team can be both exciting and a little scary. Of course, being prepared will help you deliver the vision in the best way possible while minimizing the fear factor for everyone.

ANNOUNCING THE PLAN

I am going to assume you have some form of regular, or semi-regular meetings already in place where you can announce the new plan and discuss the items you wish to co-create with your team. Whether you currently meet weekly, monthly, or even quarterly, use this meeting to set the foundation for your huddles. This will most likely be the first time the team will hear about changes to the schedule, so prepare for some pushback here. The important thing to realize is that changing the schedule will sound like the team is "losing" freedom when they first hear about it. Plus, they will likely have legitimate concerns which require a little time to figure out. Make sure to give an appropriate amount of time between announcing the plan and actually starting the new schedule for team members to adjust appropriately. Team members may need a couple of weeks or even a month to make new childcare arrangements or figure out a new transportation method. The key here is to be sensitive to the fact that this will be a change to their existing comfortable routine. One of the best ways to offset this feeling of resistance is to tell the team what's in it for them, so make sure you have thought through how you will explain the benefits of the huddle.

Explaining to your team how this will benefit them could be the difference between massive pushback and excitement to try something new. Of course, what inspires each team member will be different, so if you haven't had individual conversations about their personal goals and desires, this might be a good place to start. Understanding what drives your team will give you amazing insight into how to shape the announcement of daily huddles. Here are just a few benefits to team members that you can incorporate into your announcement:

> **Added Support** – For the team members that are currently struggling with overwhelm, or that are task saturated, a mechanism to allow for more support from the team or the leadership could be the exact benefit to turn resisters into supporters of the daily huddle. Each day will bring another opportunity for team members to ask for support, or offer support to others. This builds and strengthens reciprocity within the team and the culture. The important aspect from the leadership role is to assure team members that asking for support is safe. Remind them that nobody will be thought of as incompetent or be at risk for losing status because they ask for support.

More Recognition/Celebration – Studies have shown that the majority of people thrive when they feel acknowledged and recognized for their work. Many prioritize being acknowledged as more important than earning more money or other commonly sought-after benefits. The thought of having daily moments to celebrate wins and be recognized for achievements will literally recharge the energy of many members of your team. Even moments where the leader can simply say "thank you for the hard work" will be appreciated and motivating to team members. It creates dopamine and oxytocin to get recognized and feel celebrated, so make sure this isn't skipped in any meeting!

Improved Communication – It's safe to say that most team challenges are due to poor communication. Daily huddles provide a ritual that will strengthen communication as a team, which fosters growth and creates a space to discover opportunities needed to recover or stay viable. Encourage team members that daily huddles generate safe, consistent communication throughout the organization. Also, reiterate that this will not be a time where the leader talks for 12-15 minutes then tells everyone to get to work. Rather, this will be a place for safe communication to *and* from the team so their voices can be heard as well. Make it clear that team members will have a chance to address challenges, present ideas, solve problems, express gratitude, and be creative in a safe space. As the leader, keep in mind that effective communication takes practice, so be patient and know you are cultivating this skill set for your team through daily huddles.

Added Focus and Clarity – This benefit will be especially welcome for teams that often don't fully understand the vision or the goals of the company. Productivity and confidence can greatly increase by communicating daily about where the team needs to stay focused to complete tasks in order to arrive at the daily goal. This also reminds everyone that what they do matters and impacts the entire organization. Finally, this can bring much-needed awareness to the roles of each team member and how they can best support others and the team.

Fewer Interruptions Throughout the Day – This may be a very encouraging benefit to team members and leaders if constant interruptions regularly impede their progress toward daily goals.

One of the greatest benefits of Intelligent Huddles™ is that leaders and team members will leak less energy by not having to stop to check emails, or follow up on things that will be discussed in the huddle. Productivity will increase as everyone connects first thing in the morning to get clarity around the daily vision, receive important announcements, and put strategies in place to support the team to do their best work—all of which reduces interruptions throughout the day.

Accelerant to Their Personal Goals – This is a great time to express how much the company relies on team members, just like the team members rely on the company. Many team members want to eliminate uncertainty from their lives and feel that their positions are stable and secure. The improvements that will happen within the team, company, and culture will allow for greater goals and aspirations to be reached within the company. As the company enjoys greater success, this will allow for greater financial freedom, security, and opportunity for the team members as well. It truly is a symbiotic relationship!

Explaining to your team how this will benefit them could be the difference between massive pushback and excitement to try something new.

While I'm sure there are many more benefits that I didn't list, as well as elements that will be unique to your organization, this is a great place to start. Showing your team how daily huddles can improve their lives, both at work and at home, will hopefully alleviate most of the feelings of loss, or resistance. Another way to reduce pushback is by allowing the team to co-create the rules of engagement.

DEVELOPING HUDDLE RULES OF ENGAGEMENT

Developing the Rules of Engagement (ROE) *with* your team is a great exercise to open the space, build trust, and co-create an essential part of the program. Allowing the team to create these rules provides a sense of ownership for the program and will be the foundation by which it operates. Co-creating ROE also removes the stigma that the rules are dictated by the leader; instead, they will be viewed as the rules of the team. This creates a feeling of shared responsibility versus top-down obedience. This is also a great way for everyone to express which behaviors they believe are needed to generate the most value during the huddles. You can simply ask your team, "What behaviors would allow everyone to get the most value out of huddles?" or "What can we commit to as a team that will be our best practices and behaviors in our huddles?" The following are some examples of common ROE I encourage teams to adopt:

- Start on time.
- Do not exceed 15 minutes.
- Follow an agenda (stay on topic).
- No food or drink.
- Everyone stands (circle or as close to a circle as possible).
- Only one person at a time speaks.
- No cell phones/distractions.
- Everyone participates.
- Provide solutions, not opinions.

- No side conversations.
- Actively listen.
- Keep the space safe (all ideas/questions/solutions/and voices respected).
- Only honest answers.

Going through this exercise with your team is powerful and empowering. Again, the list above is a place to start, or generate ideas, for you and your team. All teams will be a little different and require rules that are a good fit for them. If you want to read more about setting ROE, one good resource is the book *Conversational Intelligence* by my mentor, Judith E. Glaser. Like I said earlier, the ROE will be the foundation that allows structure and order for your huddles. Since ROE establishes a foundation and creates team member ownership of the program, this is one of the first steps that should be accomplished—either when you announce the plan, or during the first official huddle. Once you have your initial list of ROE, print and post them so they are visible wherever you plan to have the huddles.

Developing the Rules of Engagement (ROE) with your team is a great exercise to open the space, build trust, and co-create an essential part of the program.

Revisit and recommit to your ROE monthly. Sometimes, the team needs to get in the flow of daily huddles before knowing which behaviors are actually needed. So, I like to consider the ROE a working document. Revisiting it monthly allows an opportunity to add or delete rules if needed to make your huddles even better.

The combination of the ROE and your agenda will allow you to facilitate the huddles with structure and consistency. However, understanding how to utilize a conversational flow within the huddle is what will take it from a standard "meeting" and convert it into valuable communication that capitalizes on all of the neuroscience and mindfulness tools you've learned up to this point.

LEAD USING A CONVERSATIONAL FLOW

Before I learned how to incorporate conversational flow into my huddles, many of my meetings would fall flat. I started off using more of a "tell, sell, yell" method of leading. I didn't really raise my voice, but I was the one who always did the talking. I would share, share, and share some more, believing that my ideas were the best. I also felt like this was my role as the leader, to push information onto my team members. Instead, this method only pushed great people away. My intention was always good, but my impact never landed consistently the way I wanted. As soon as I would begin to dominate the meeting, pushing endless amounts of information, I would see team members' eyes glaze over and sense their imaginations shutting down; it was clear they lost sight of the big picture.

Most of you reading this book already know if you have made the same mistake. If you're unsure, one way to know if you've fallen into this trap is to ask yourself, *Do I regularly have to repeat myself over and over, but the information never seems to sink in with my team members?* This is definitely a sign that a leader is pushing information too much and not utilizing a conversational flow. Don't beat yourself up about it … it's not your fault! This is probably the first time you've heard about conversational flow in a meeting, so let me explain a little more about how to use this technique.

Everything on this planet has duality—light and dark, good and evil, up and down. Duality in a conversation is simply "push" and "pull" energy. When you tell something to another individual, that is you pushing energy to them. Asking questions of your team would be pulling energy (answers, ideas, and solutions) from them. A perfect example is announcing your plan to start daily huddles. You will need to push your plan to the team and explain the benefits they can expect. Then, you can pull information from them by asking for their thoughts. Are they excited and believe in the vision? Could they add brilliant ideas to make the outcome (and their buy-in) even greater? Keeping a healthy balance of push and pull energy during your huddle is what creates the conversational flow.

Using a conversational flow is significantly more effective for team members compared to processing data being pushed from one speaker.

Conversations feel less formal and allow energy to flow easily. They bring team members to a place where they are ready to engage their minds. When you prime the conversational space for trust and make the huddle flow consistent, you will experience the type of conversations that spark ideas and energize creativity. Using a conversational flow is significantly more effective for team members compared to processing data being pushed from one speaker. Also, the democratic nature of a conversation allows each team member to weigh in, increasing the feeling of ownership around the topic being discussed. The most brilliant ideas, trust, and accountability show up when you can create, share, and discover equally from each other!

The easiest way to start a conversation during a huddle is to ask a question to which you do not know the answer. If there is a challenge you want the team to provide ideas or co-create solutions around, ask about that. If there isn't anything pressing to resolve, ask a discovery question such as, "What is one way you think we leak energy throughout the day, and how could we guide the situation to a new, or positive outcome?" Or, you may ask something a little more personal such as, "Tell me something you aspire to achieve this year." Ultimately, the balanced exchange of push and pull energy is more important than the specific questions you ask, so don't worry about getting it wrong. Finally, team members are more likely to listen, connect, and allow themselves to be influenced if there is no judgement around their answers. This may seem obvious, but psychological safety depends on everyone feeling confident about speaking up. Stay consistent and you will find a flow that works for you and your team. One challenge you may run into, however, is getting everyone to participate—especially if they don't initially see the value huddles provide.

RECOGNIZING AND DEALING WITH PUSHBACK

Everyone deals with change differently, so don't be surprised if you notice some pushback after starting the huddle program. I would love to tell you that all pushback disappears if you do huddles for a month, or six months, or a year. This simply isn't the case because the resolution depends on both the team members and the leader working through the process together. If someone isn't feeling the value of the huddle, doing more of them will not change their mind. This is why it's important to recognize and address pushback very early in the program, or anytime you notice it starting to creep in for that matter.

There is always an underlying cause for the resistance that you must discover. It could be that an individual is simply lost in their excuses. This is often the case when you experience pushback around changing the schedule. People who don't consider themselves "morning people" will not be excited about showing up twenty minutes earlier to work. Some people may not understand the vision and feel like huddles will only take more time from their day when they could be getting stuff done. Or, if huddles are new to the team, there could be some uncertainty around the unknown. Regardless of the reason that created the opposition, pushback is totally normal and can almost always be remedied.

It may sound strange, but pushback is actually a gift that will allow you to create something even better than you initially imagined. It provides a chance to be curious and ask questions. Pushback also allows you to include team members in the process right from the beginning, which demonstrates that you really do want (and need) their input. By pulling in the voices of those who aren't fully aligned with your plan, you can demonstrate the power of co-creating solutions. When team members know you have heard them, and see you put effort into applying solutions that were created together, it will build a level of trust and a feeling of partnership from the beginning. This is, after all, one of the reasons to start huddles in the first place!

Pushback is actually a gift that will allow you to create something even better than you initially imagined.

Pushback also allows you to practice the mindfulness techniques of controlling your own responses. It's totally normal to feel like pushback against the huddle is something personal against the leader. I can say that this is actually very rare and it's almost always more about the team member who's resisting than it is about you. So the first rule when dealing with pushback is to not take it personally. A leader cannot get to the bottom of the real problem while responding emotionally. Awareness of your own emotions will help you determine if you can calmly and objectively have a conversation on the spot, or if you may need to take some time before addressing the issue. No matter what, keep up with the awareness exercises from Chapter 4 and don't be upset if some team members aren't aligned right away. Remember, pushback is a gift! Before you can deal with opposition, however, you need to be able to recognize when it happens. So, what are some ways team members may exhibit pushback?

The most common way team members demonstrate pushback is by not participating or staying engaged during the huddle. Watch for people who never raise their hand or volunteer to answer questions. Try to pick up on nonverbal body cues such as folded arms, inadvertent facial expressions, and avoiding eye contact. Negative gestures such as eye-rolls or shaking their head back and forth to indicate they don't agree when the leader discusses a plan or new idea could also be indications of opposition. These signs may highlight when a team member is revealing pushback, but could also be the actions of someone who is shy or introverted and isn't comfortable in the group setting yet. Knowing your team and having an awareness of individual personalities will help you determine who is resisting and who is simply out of their comfort zone.

The best way to deal with someone who isn't participating is to simply ask them why. I find that calling someone out in the middle of a huddle can be too aggressive and put them into the primitive, defensive part of their brain. This is the exact opposite of what you want, so this should be avoided. Instead of highlighting someone specifically, I recommend reminding the team that part of the huddle ROE states everyone needs to participate. Then, set up a time with the team member who isn't engaging to have a private conversation.

Discussing the matter one-on-one is usually way more productive and allows you to focus on just them and their struggle with participating in huddles. I like to start the conversation by emphasizing that they are in a safe space to express themselves and there will be no judgement on their answers. The intent is to improve the huddle and bring more value to everyone, so they should feel free to speak candidly. I avoid questions that insinuate the team member is wrong, such as, "Why can't you get on board?" or "What's your problem during the huddles?" Instead, try to focus on open-ended questions that really help get to the root. Here are some questions that have worked well for me in the past:

Help me understand what would need to happen for you to participate more in the huddles?

What would you add to our huddles that would help them feel more valuable to you?

What is one aspiration of yours that huddles might be able to bring into your reality sooner?

The questions help move a person into the productive part of their brain while giving the leader a treasure trove of information. The first question highlights where the team member is stuck and starts to pull solutions as to what they believe may be a remedy. The problem can then be brought into the huddle to get the team's opinion as to what a solution could be. This is where people start to come alive and use their creativity. Next, by asking how to make the huddle more valuable you get a better feeling about what is important to that team member. You find out what motivates them! The best leaders know what drives each team member so they can pull the most out of them. Finally, asking about their aspirations and how huddles can accelerate those results causes them to connect one of their dreams with huddles. This helps the team member personalize what they will get out of huddles and see it as a mechanism to move them toward success.

Another common way a team member demonstrates pushback is by questioning "why" you are discussing something instead of asking "how" to be successful around the topic. Questions that focus on "why" means that there's some sort of conflict in their mind, or confusion as to the benefits. This is one type of pushback that is okay to address on the spot because others may also be confused or conflicted, but not speaking up. Any confusion around the vision needs to be clarified with the team to ensure everyone knows what they are working towards. The best results cannot be realized without clarity. Likewise, identifying conflict as early as possible will keep a challenge from growing out of control. Get the entire team involved generating ideas that would eliminate the conflict and determining what the first step would look like to make it a reality.

> *Any confusion around the vision needs to be clarified with the team to ensure everyone knows what they are working towards.*

Another form of pushback is when a team member is consistently late to huddles. Stick to your ROE and start every huddle on time. Do not wait for people to arrive if they are not on time, as this can quickly spiral out of control. It also sends the unintended message to those who *are* present that their time is less valuable. This is another situation where I would refresh everyone on the ROE, then set up a time for a private conversation with the team member who is unable to be on time. Again, asking the team member why they are having trouble being at work on time will reveal most of what you need to know. In my experience this is usually one of three things: 1) the team member needs help establishing a nighttime and morning routine to set them up for success; 2) the team member has some legitimate challenge that they cannot control such as dropping a child off at school or daycare; or 3) they are rebelling against the earlier schedule and think that by disrupting the huddle you will give up on it. In the case of 1 and 2, there is usually a solution that is fairly easy to develop and the resistance will resolve when it is put in place. The third issue, however, is when hard conversations may have to happen to determine if the team member is the right fit.

Sometimes, pushback cannot be resolved with some simple questions, or by bringing the challenge to the team for a solution. Sometimes, the alignment between your vision for the team and a specific team member just isn't possible. This is another thing huddles can reveal sooner than later, so if the first set of questions doesn't seem like it will yield a possible solution, then you may need to ask the team member if they really want to be a part of the team. Explain that the culture you envision for the team and the company is one that requires respect of others, respect for the schedule, and full participation. If that isn't something they can align with, the only option left is separation. If possible, do what you can to support them with a healthy transition off of the team and into a new role. I always recommend keeping emotions out of this discussion; work hard to part as friends so you don't burn the bridge. You never know when a team member may go to another company, learn new skills or gain maturity, then come back to be an amazing asset for your team later on.

Ultimately, pushback is normal and does not mean you are doing something wrong. The key to dealing with pushback is to be patient with yourself and your team. Stay committed to your "why" and your vision to grow the culture and team in a healthy way. Keep working through the process and utilize the pushback to create an even better daily huddle than you imagined. Pushback almost always softens if you stay consistent, ask questions, and continuously cultivate value.

CHAPTER TAKEAWAYS

It is normal and completely understandable to have some anxiety around bringing something new to your team. As exciting as the possibilities are, it's human nature to fear change. The three sections in this chapter were all intended to boost your confidence as you set out to launch daily huddles. What I think is so valuable about this information is that it helps remove some of the unknown and equips you to handle situations that could cause some leaders to give up, or worse yet, not even start. The following are the four main takeaways from this chapter that will accelerate you toward success with huddles.

1. When you announce the plan to start daily huddles, put an

emphasis on the benefits to the team. It's much easier for team members to get behind something new if they know what's in it for them early on.

2. Co-create the ROE with your team at the announcement, or during the first couple of huddles. This gets them involved providing weigh-in to increase their buy-in. Helping to create the rules generates more ownership and personal accountability for the program.

3. Huddles should feel more like a conversation than a data-dump. The whole point of huddles is to increase effective communication, productivity, growth, build trust, and improve the culture. You can't achieve any of that without utilizing push and pull energy with your team.

4. Embrace team member pushback as the gift that it is. It is almost never personal, so don't take it personally and know that there is usually a solution to eliminate the pushback. Get curious and co-create even better relationships to work through challenges.

Putting the tips, techniques, and tools provided up to this point into practice will absolutely give you a significant advantage over a leader who tries to start a huddle program on their own. Not only will you fare better than most, I am confident to say you have the best chance to succeed! You are equipped already with the tools necessary to launch and run daily huddles, but how will you know if they're working? How can you measure the effectiveness of your Intelligent Huddles™?

CHAPTER 7

Measuring Huddle Success

You can't really know where you are going until you know where you have been.

—**Maya Angelou**

One of the most encouraging things about huddles is when you start to see results. However, as Maya Angelou states above, you need to know where you've been (and where you are) before you can truly recognize where you are going. I have stated throughout this book how huddles can improve your business, including overall performance and culture, but sometimes the changes are subtle at first. You will need a good way to establish baselines and track changes so you can see the progress being made. Or, just as important, to see where progress isn't being made.

The first section of this chapter will review some of the information dealing with key performance indicators (KPIs) and how they are critical to keeping tabs on the performance of the organization. But one of the largest impacts to the company and team performance is how strong the culture is among the team members. So along with the KPI review, I will discuss some Culture Performance Indicators (CPIs) and how to score your team so you can find a culture baseline score. Remember, you have to know where you've been and where you are before you can know where you're going. This baseline score will also be how you measure progress and determine if huddles are improving your culture over time. Finally, I will cover some of the most common mistakes I see when leaders implement a daily huddle for the first time. This section isn't just for newbies though—it can also be a great reference for those who have been working huddles for some time and want to know why they aren't as effective as they should be.

I have no doubt that if you follow the procedures I've outlined in the book so far, you will notice significant improvements in reaching company aspirations, strengthening culture, and achieving company and team member goals. That said, the best motivator is to see for yourself how the organization changes over time.

TRACKING THE SUCCESS OF DAILY HUDDLES

Think back to the section in Chapter 4 about getting clear on company vision, goals, and aspirations. Did you write them down? Are they visible where you and the entire team can see them? These aspirations are one of the reasons, or the *why*, behind implementing huddles in the first place. They are also how you can measure whether or not huddles are improving your team, and your company. Hopefully you've been tracking the best KPIs to determine your progress toward these goals for some time now. If not, now is the time to start! You may be able to pull the history of certain KPIs, such as team member retention, revenue, or other financials. Others you may only have real-time data. No matter what, you need to draw a line in the sand to say, "This is where we started."

Most goals will fall into one of three categories: performance, revenue, or culture. In most cases an improvement in performance will also improve revenue. However, you may miss key parts of the story if all you focus on is hitting a financial number. There are many other opportunities that will reveal themselves based on what you track, so I highly recommend getting as specific as possible. Instead of just tracking goals, the most effective process is to track KPIs that indicate movement in relation to your goals.

> *No matter what, you need to draw a line in the sand to say, "This is where we started."*

For instance, we could focus on monthly revenue in our salon in order to hit an annual goal. But this is a trailing indicator, meaning it only tells us how we did after the month is done. There's nothing we can do to impact that number. However, if we choose to focus on a leading indicator, like pre-booking clients for their next appointment, we can more accurately predict revenue for the upcoming month. This tells a much more specific story and gives us a chance to impact the next month. This also gives each of our stylists a way to predict their revenue for the next month which adds stability to their lives.

Once you have identified the best KPIs to track for your goals, the next step is to find the baseline number to measure the next few months against. I recommend using a minimum of three months' worth of data before considering the baseline reliable. Finding the baseline for your KPI is pretty straightforward because you simply determine the average over a three-month period. If you have six months' worth of data, this is even better as it will include elements such as seasonal fluctuations, and balance out data that isn't typical. Going back to the example of pre-booking clients, I would determine my baseline by calculating the following:

Month 1 – Total pre-bookings = 65%
Month 2 – Total pre-bookings = 59%
Month 3 – Total pre-bookings = 72%

My baseline for pre-bookings would be the average of the three months, or (65+59+72)/3, which is 65.33%.

Again, if you have longer-term data it will increase the accuracy of your baseline. But if you haven't been tracking KPIs, three months will give you a good foundation. Now, write this number on a tracking board that can be used to measure how the team does each day, week, and month to determine if the revenue goal will be achieved, or if a recovery plan may be necessary to achieve monthly goals.

Of course, there will most likely be additional KPIs to track to provide a more complete picture, but this gives you the idea. Also, you may want to see how your baseline compares to industry standards for specific KPIs, if they are known.

Determining a baseline and measuring KPIs works great for tracking revenue and performance goals. However, tracking improvement in company culture can be a little more difficult. Typical KPIs don't translate well to culture goals, so how do we establish a culture baseline without over-complicating things?

ESTABLISHING A CULTURE BASELINE

I define a company's culture as the shared values and behaviors embodied by the entire organization. A people-oriented leadership style, trusting and safe environment, elevated but realistic expectations, and working toward a common vision are typical elements of a company with a strong culture. This type of atmosphere tends to attract and retain the best workers, encourage innovation and creativity, and create a tribe-like feeling for team members. Once established, the culture is demonstrated by the attitudes and actions of everyone in the company and often determines the strength of the relationship among the team and between the team and the leadership.

Deliberately crafting the culture you want your organization to embody is vital for top performance and organizational success. According to research conducted by Grant Thornton, one of the world's leading organizations of independent audit, tax and advisory firms, "An organization's culture and health is just as reliable a predictor of success as sales figures and needs to be measured."[1] The challenge lies in establishing metrics to accurately measure culture. The research by Grant Thornton further revealed, "A staggering 69% of executives have not established [culture] metrics which they track."[2] Based on this research, I can't argue that defining perfect metrics isn't a challenge. The good news is, we don't need perfect metrics to determine if huddles are improving our culture. We only need indicators ... Culture Performance Indicators (CPIs), to be exact.

Deliberately crafting the culture you want your organization to embody is vital for top performance and organizational success.

Before you can choose which CPIs to track, you need to be able to meaningfully describe the ideal culture for your organization. Develop a clear definition that is a balance between company values and vision, and a desirable team member experience. Then you can use this definition to choose CPIs that indicate whether reality reflects the ideal. Below is a list of twenty-five CPIs that you can choose from to establish your culture baseline.

1. Trust
2. Opportunity for Growth
3. Clear Communication

4. Work-Life Balance
5. Proper Tools/Training
6. Innovative Environment
7. Recognition
8. Understand Role
9. Appropriate Responsibility
10. Fun
11. Opportunity to Advance
12. Safe to Give Feedback
13. Teamwork
14. Flexible and Adaptable
15. Respect
16. Safety
17. Joyful
18. Stress/Overwhelm
19. Support
20. Feedback is Helpful
21. Feel Heard
22. Retention
23. Sense of Community
24. Value Alignment
25. Team Member Participation

Based on the chosen CPIs that represent your ideal culture, now you must determine if reality matches the ideal. Leadership should prioritize collecting this information and setting a baseline just like with performance and revenue goals—and the most effective way to establish this baseline is through a company culture survey.

A company culture survey is a tool to collect feedback directly from team members. The information can be used to assess what the team members think about the culture, whether they relate to it or not, and what can be improved to make the organization a better place to work. Creating and administering a survey that yields quality, actionable answers can be a bit of an art form, so here is some general guidance to make sure you are successful.

The first, unbreakable rule for administering a company culture survey is that it *must* be anonymous. This rule is especially important if trust isn't one of the main attributes of the current culture. Team members may not feel safe to express their true feelings and concerns if they think there may be ramifications. So this rule should never be broken, or you may not get the truth about where you are. Similarly, don't take it personally if the responses to these questions aren't great. The first time around there will probably be some enlightening information that doesn't necessarily reflect on you. Instead, use the answers to identify core problems and bring them into your huddles to co-create solutions to make improvements.

You don't want to overwhelm team members with a huge, time-consuming survey. Pick some of the most important areas of the culture that you want to use as your baseline and start with those. Limiting your survey to ten to twenty questions will provide an accurate picture of where the culture stands without taking too much time out of your team members' day. Similarly, allow time for solutions to be implemented and changes to take hold before administering the survey again. Depending on the progress of your huddles, three to six months after establishing the baseline should be adequate. It's fairly common to ask for new feedback twice per year.

Finally, I recommend that every question have two parts: a rating scale so you can associate a "score" with each answer; and, a space where team members can provide specific data or suggestions. Each question should be clearly worded in a way that stimulates specific answers. It should be made clear to team members that complete answers are the best way to get their voice heard, especially for questions where the rating was low. Here are five examples of questions that meet these criteria:

Rate the following questions/statements on a scale from 1 to 5, with 1 meaning you strongly disagree, and 5 meaning you strongly agree.

1. Does leadership do a good job of recognizing you for your accomplishments?

1   2   3   4   5

Why or why not?

2. Do you have the time, tools, and training to do your job well?

1   2   3   4   5

What would you need to do your job better?

3. Do you feel like you can provide feedback to leadership without consequence?

1   2   3   4   5

Why or why not?

4. Does your company provide a psychologically safe working environment for all employees?

1   2   3   4   5

Why or why not?

5. Do you see yourself working for this company long-term?

1   2   3   4   5

Why or why not?

Again, this is just a very short sample of the type of questions that can be included on a company culture survey. The full survey should consist of ten to twenty questions on various topics to construct a complete picture of the organization's culture. Each survey question should tie directly to one of the chosen CPIs in order to measure reality against the ideal.

Once all team members have completed the survey, find the average score for each answer. This will reveal strengths and weaknesses among the CPIs you want to track. Next, total the average scores for all the questions and divide by the number of questions to determine the baseline culture score.

Here's an example:

You administer a company culture survey to 10 team members. Each survey has 20 questions.

First, calculate the average score for each question by adding all scores for question 1 and dividing by the number of team members (in this example, 10). Then do the same for question 2, and so on.

>Question 1 average = 3.5

>Question 2 average = 4.2

>Question 3 average = 2.4

>...

>Question 20 average = 4.0

Next, add all of the average scores and divide by the total number of questions (in this example, 20) to determine the Baseline Culture Score (BCS).

$$BCS = (3.5 + 4.2 + 2.4 + etc. + 4.0) / 20 = 3.53$$

I wanted to provide another resource for you, so I have developed a basic culture survey that you can use to establish your baseline. All you have to do is pick the questions that best match your chosen CPIs and delete the others. Feel free to get creative and make up some of your own questions as well. You can download the survey template at www.dreahemmer.com/huddleresources.

I am sorry for not warning you that there would be some math! I promise, once you do this once or twice it will all make sense and you will have great baseline references to measure how daily huddles are impacting your performance, revenue, and culture goals. You should see improvements in all three, but this isn't always the case. There are a few common mistakes that I see fairly often that can drastically reduce the results that intelligent huddles normally provide.

COMMON MISTAKES
Not Being Consistent

One of the most important rules for succeeding with huddles is that they must happen consistently, on time, every day. Leaders that haven't fully committed to huddles, or the behaviors required to be successful with huddles, may struggle to stay consistent. Part of the problem with skipping huddles here and there, or not starting on time, is that team members stop taking them seriously. Once the team starts to lose their dedication to huddles, they begin losing progress toward goals. Huddles can be such an amazing opportunity for a team and a company, but the leader has to be committed. Remember, successful huddles start at the top. If you find yourself making this mistake, remind yourself why you were excited to start huddles in the first place. Re-read Chapter 4 to refresh yourself on establishing the best mindset. The rest of the team will follow your lead, so prioritize being consistent for the best results.

Not Giving Huddles Time to Work

Huddles can drastically improve the trajectory of an organization, but like anything, it takes a little time. I've seen many leaders start huddles with a lot of motivation and enthusiasm, only to get a week or two in and realize they take work and dedication. It's very common for humans to want to see progress from the hard work we put in, and then get impatient if we don't see immediate results. Huddles take some time to work, especially if there is a little pushback at first. Give huddles a minimum of three months before trying to figure out if they are changing your business and commit to sticking with them for a minimum of six months. Trust your KPIs and CPIs and stay consistent. You *will* start to see positive results.

Give huddles a minimum of three months before trying to figure out if they are changing your business and commit to sticking with them for a minimum of six months.

Giving In to Pushback

Trying new things will almost always feel uncomfortable at first, and not everyone will be supportive in the beginning. Change is hard for everyone, especially when team members believe they are comfortable right where they are. However, as a leader with a vision for taking your team and company to the highest level, you have to be aware of how damaging it can be to give in to pushback.

Pushback may show up in the form of pressure to reduce the number of huddles (consistency), being too relaxed with the ROE, flexing the start time until everyone shows up, or not addressing disruptive members or members that skip huddles. No matter how the pushback shows up, it must be dealt with. Explain to the team again why you implemented huddles and the benefits they bring to the team and the company. Remind team members how they can personally benefit from huddles as well. And, if necessary, be prepared to have the hard conversation about whether they are a good fit with the organization and the culture you hope to create. There is a difference between listening to feedback and caving to pushback. You must be stronger than the excuses of those who resist.

Not Utilizing Conversational Flow

The quickest way to break trust and create silos in your huddles is by pushing information without pulling ideas and energy from your team as well. Just because you are leading the huddles doesn't mean you should be the only one participating. One major lesson that I learned was that my ideas aren't always the best. My business began to grow in so many ways when I pulled the best ideas and thinking from my team instead of pushing only my own. Research has shown the "tell, sell, yell" method almost always leads to high turnover, low trust, silos of information, unmet goals, low participation, very little accountability, and leadership burnout. Go back and review Chapter 2 for the basics of neuroscience and Chapter 6 for facilitating with conversational flow. When you utilize push-and-pull conversations with your team you will see that the sum of the team's intelligence is significantly greater than the individual parts. Capitalize on this benefit as it is the foundation of intelligent huddles.

Never Starting

I see this time and time again. I will host a workshop with a leader, or group of leaders, discussing all the things that a daily huddle could do for their business. The leader is *so* inspired and feels they have what it takes to bring this information back to their team and start a successful daily huddle program. I wish it only took that first bit of motivation to make huddles successful, but our minds, old habits, and resistance from our team can create a perfect storm to cast doubt and remove motivation. Even though leaders know huddles are the best tool to support the team, improve the culture, and achieve their goals, they get scared and never start. You have to plan for this and make sure you are stronger than your fears. I have provided the tools to prepare, launch, and facilitate intelligent huddles in this book. Yes, you will make mistakes. Yes, there will be pushback and challenges. Yes, it will take work up front. However, once you start to overcome some of these barriers, you will start to see the victories and achieve goals, then huddles will start to get really fun. But you have to start.

Allowing Too Many Distractions

After consulting with a company to help them start their huddle program, I will often observe some of their huddles to see if there are opportunities to improve. One of the things I notice over and over is that they allow too many distractions. This is usually caused by not developing a complete set of ROE, or not enforcing them. It may not seem like a big deal at first to allow food, drinks, or cell phones, but allowing these distractions will constantly drain energy from the huddle. One of the keys to success for huddles is that the team is present and focused on the content. The best solution for this common mistake is to avoid it from the beginning by establishing a complete set of ROE. Review Chapter 6, which provides a list of the most useful rules I've learned over the last decade. Creating and enforcing a thorough set of ROE supports best practices and behaviors to make huddles valuable for everyone, so don't allow distractions to rob you and your team of the amazing benefits.

Not Being Prepared

The last mistake that I see way too often is leaders trying to run a huddle without preparing. Yes, the agenda will help keep you focused and guide you through the topics. But leaders need to take some time before the huddle to review the KPIs that will be discussed, talk with team members about victories, and put some thought into the piece of magic they choose to close the huddle. Also, if you know you will have someone present a section of the huddle, make sure they are prepared as well. Help them to deliver their presentation with confidence. When a huddle is executed well and flows as intended, it is the best catalyst for creating energy to start everyone's day. However, showing up unprepared and stumbling through the huddle can actually drain energy. Nobody expects you to be perfect leading every huddle, but you can always be prepared and do your best.

CHAPTER TAKEAWAYS

The act of having a daily huddle will not change your business alone. How you facilitate the huddles, track key information, and use the information to develop ideas and create solutions is what will bring amazing improvements to your business. One of the keys to making this possible is establishing an accurate baseline for where you are so you can measure the progress of where you want to go.

One of the most important takeaways from this chapter is be specific with what you track. I totally understand that almost everyone wants their business to make more money. However, tracking revenue is a broad metric that only tells part of the story. What are the KPIs that lead to revenue? Which actions and systems can you track that cause revenue to happen in a predictable manner? When you track more specific elements of your business you will start to see which cogs are working and which ones need to be adjusted. This level of detail can't be seen if the tracking metric is too broad.

Make sure to choose KPIs that indicate movement in relation to your goals. Pick one or two KPIs per goal to track and make improvements around. Running a business and leading a team is a marathon, not a sprint. Trying to track and change too many variables at once will typically be less effective and can lead to burnout. Establish a solid baseline for each KPI and co-create ideas and solutions for growth within the huddles. This is where the magic happens.

How you facilitate the huddles, track key information, and use the information to develop ideas and create solutions is what will bring amazing improvements to your business.

Setting a baseline for where an organization's culture is compared to the ideal you want it to be can be a little trickier. However, I shared some of the most common elements (CPIs) that can impact culture and provided a method to establish a useful baseline. Just like with performance and revenue, goals centered around culture require an understanding of what you want your culture to be. This may seem obvious, but take some time to develop a definition of what the ideal culture is, then set goals to work toward achieving that. Again, pick one or two CPIs that best represent each goal, then develop a company culture survey to establish the baseline. This will tell you the strengths and weaknesses of the culture so you can bring them to the huddle and develop systems and a plan for improvement. Don't forget to download the survey template from www.dreahemmer.com/huddleresources.

Finally, I would love to tell you that running a daily huddle will be a breeze and you will never face any challenges. This simply isn't the case. Every team is unique and dynamic, and will have its own set of challenges. However, none of them are insurmountable. I have provided the tools throughout this book to set you up for success. Most of these tools have been developed over time by overcoming my own hard-learned lessons. Study the most common mistakes before you launch your daily huddles so you can have awareness when things like pushback, or impatience start to creep in. The fact that you're reading this book means you have what it takes to succeed and I know you will. I believe in you and I'm here to help!

I'm excited for you to turn the page and read the final chapter of this book. The conclusion will not only reinforce some of the most important elements presented in the book, but will provide some additional tools to help you succeed with Intelligent Huddles™.

CHAPTER 8

Conclusion

"The secret of getting ahead is getting started."

—**Mark Twain**

You started reading this book because you know something within your organization needs to change. Maybe your team is capable of performing at the highest level, but nothing has coaxed the excellence out of them yet. Maybe you have hit a plateau in your business and just can't seem to break through to the next level of growth. Or perhaps you are exhausted as the team leader, working way too hard to keep your team on track and you need a better way to lead. Whatever the reason, I know Intelligent Huddles™ can help you and your organization.

Typical organizations do not provide training on how to run an effective daily meeting. Nor is it something that is taught in business school or during a project management certification. Most leaders simply mimic the facilitator that came before them, whether they were good or not. It is this gap in training that lead me to write this book.

Some of you were skeptical when you first started reading because you have tried daily huddles before and they didn't produce the results I have claimed. I get it. You may still be skeptical, but let me assure you that the Intelligent Huddle™ system is very different than your typical daily huddle. The incorporation of neuroscience principles and conversational flow, as well as understanding your own mindset, are game-changers that will supercharge your huddles and create massive opportunity for improvement.

The education necessary to be successful with Intelligent Huddles™ is all here in these pages. I have honed this knowledge for more than a decade, both in my own business and by coaching other business owners and team leaders. It may seem like a lot to implement at first, but if you take it one chapter at a time you will see that this process is absolutely achievable. I promise you, the hardest part of the process is getting started. You must get past the fear section of your brain and take the first step. As the Mark Twain quote above so clearly states, getting started is the secret to getting ahead. To help simplify the information presented in this book and make it even easier to get started, I've distilled many of the key principles into an easy to remember framework.

FRAMEWORK TO FACILITATE HUDDLES

There was a lot of information presented in this book and some of you probably feel a little overwhelmed. I completely understand that feeling and have been where you are right now. First, let me reassure you that nobody gets it right immediately. It's a process that you will have to stay committed to, work through, and become more confident with before you can really feel comfortable running an Intelligent Huddle™. This is true for most things, so don't get down

Conclusion

on yourself if it takes a few weeks to really find your groove. Just keep reviewing the concepts and stay consistent. Because I've been where you are and want to help minimize the overwhelm, I developed the acronym CONNECT to help you remember the key principles of the Intelligent Huddle™.

C – Conversational Flow

O – Opportunity

N – Neuroscience

N – Needs

E – Engagement

C – Commitment

T – Trust

Conversational Flow: Keeping a healthy balance of push and pull energy during your huddle is what creates the conversational flow. This informal style allows energy to exchange more easily and encourages team members to tap into ideas and creativity, rather than just process data. Additionally, when team members contribute they feel more ownership, which creates higher accountability, a desire to perform at a higher level, and trust among the team.

One key to success for utilizing conversational flow is to have self-awareness around how you are showing up to the huddle. Being mindful of your own emotions, reactions, and words is key to demonstrating to your team that the space is psychologically safe. You have to become aware of how you're showing up every day and the energy you are bringing to the huddle since your team will be taking their cue from you.

Opportunities: One of the biggest benefits of daily Intelligent Huddles™ is how many opportunities will be revealed. These may show up in the form of a challenge that needs to be solved, a place where energy is leaking, or a team member sharing an innovative way to improve performance, just to name a few. Listen for complaints that come up more than once, or try to notice when energy shifts among the team around certain topics. Regardless of what is being discussed, any conversation can lead to opportunity... as long as you are consciously listening for it. You could even assign someone to specifically listen for opportunities and read them back to the team at the end of the huddle. If something strikes a chord with the team, it can be added as a discussion point for following huddles.

> *Regardless of what is being discussed, any conversation can lead to opportunity... as long as you are consciously listening for it.*

Just as important as identifying opportunities to improve is identifying opportunities to celebrate. As discussed earlier, this is one of the most important elements to move team members into the better part of their brains and is how I recommend starting every huddle. Opportunities to celebrate translate into opportunities to prepare your team to be in the best part of their minds to start their day. This can increase efficiency, productivity, and creativity, so don't miss out on this huge opportunity!

Neuroscience: One of the most important elements that makes my daily huddle system "intelligent" is that it incorporates a basic understanding of neuroscience. You are empowered with the ability to recognize when stress responses are happening and cortisol is being created during a conversation. Likewise, you can also employ techniques to down-regulate the cortisol and up-regulate oxytocin instead.

Down-regulation of cortisol happens by minimizing fear, uncertainty, and other stress-inducing elements. Up-regulating oxytocin can be done by ensuring you and other participants are inclusive, appreciative, and foster new ideas and possibilities. Being able to change a person's state from defensive, isolating, and fearful to collaborative, participating, and creative is a superpower that no leader should be without.

Needs: One of the most important points to cover during each huddle is the "needs" for the day. What does the company need? What does the team need? And, what does each team member need to be successful for the day? This is a great place for people to ask for support, discuss where systems are being interrupted, and highlight which parts of the day may require extra planning to ensure success.

> *What does the company need? What does the team need? And, what does each team member need to be successful for the day?*

Be careful not to look too far into the future during your huddles. In order to keep them on time, you will need to prioritize what is needed for that day to succeed. This doesn't mean you can't share and discover new ideas together, or bring up topics that may take more time to discuss. If that happens, reassure the team that they have brought up a really important topic and even though there isn't time to discuss it now, it can be the focus during another huddle or at a monthly or quarterly meeting.

Engagement: Strive for maximum engagement from the team during each huddle. Ideally, every team member should talk or participate at least once. By getting every team member engaged at some point it creates a sense of belonging in the tribe. When people feel like they belong and contribute to something that is bigger than themselves, they hold themselves and others accountable and work with a sense of purpose. This sense of purpose is critical to maintaining a positive emotional environment and helps team members understand how they fit into the big picture. Engagement starts in the daily huddle and helps develop team members that are involved, productive, and understand they are working toward both their own goals *and* the goals of the company.

Commitment: Commit to sticking to the huddle agenda as well as starting and ending on time. This simple display of consistency will set the example for the team when you ask them for commitments to the organization. The commitment to staying on time also ensures that you are respecting the team's time.

The other commitment I need you to make is giving huddles time to work. No program instantly fixes an organization that needs to change, and huddles are no different. It is a process that may take a few months to really get into a good, productive flow. Commit to a minimum of six months of daily Intelligent Huddles™. Use the techniques already covered to keep a good flow each day, and track the changes to your KPIs and culture. I have yet to see an organization fail to make drastic improvements when they follow my method, but you will need to be committed and give it a little time.

Trust: Trust is essential to high-performing organizations, and like engagement, it is most easily developed through a strong daily huddle. Having open conversations with team members and being receptive to what they have to say improves organizational trust. This, in turn, creates a culture that team members want to come to every day and even influences their willingness to go above and beyond in their roles. Utilizing Intelligent Huddles™ to upregulate oxytocin, have conversations, and improve communication provides the perfect environment to build and maintain trust.

Make sure you CONNECT with your team every day. This simple framework should help you remember the key principles of the Intelligent Huddle™ system. That said, I encourage you to go back from time to time and review different chapters to refresh yourself on some of the deeper concepts and explanations.

FINAL THOUGHTS

In the introduction to this book, I asked if your organization could close the doors for nearly two months, then come back together and implement new requirements and policies, retain every team member, and operate as if you never skipped a beat with just hours of notice? While I'm sure there were some exceptions, most businesses did not fare quite this well—if they survived at all. I didn't ask that question to make you feel bad, or to brag about how great our company was. I asked it so you would honestly evaluate the strength of your organization, and, to show you that a system does exist that is so powerful it allows you to thrive when the unexpected arrives.

The purpose of this book is to give you access to that system. One you can use every day that will build the type of culture you need to retain team members, even during hard times. A tool that provides the time and space for critical communication that will provide clarity to your team and inspire them to be their best before starting each day. A process that will spark creativity, innovation, trust, and participation from everyone on the team so they feel like they belong in the tribe. And a safety net that allows your team to thrive, even when unexpected curveballs show up. It may sound like a tall order, but all of this and more is absolutely possible by implementing Intelligent Huddles™.

Using the Intelligent Huddle™ method, you will see an increase in productivity, revenue, team engagement, organizational trust, and the strength of your company's culture. You will notice a decrease in time required to communicate to your team, less stress about daily tasks, and less employee turnover. Your team will be more involved with the business and become accountable for meeting personal and company goals.

Now, take a second to celebrate yourself right now for finishing this book! That alone is a major accomplishment in today's busy society.

It was also the first step to implementing Intelligent Huddles™ in your organization. Now, the next step is to get yourself in the right mindset and start preparing your space. So, what are you waiting for? The only thing standing between you and your greatest aspirations is getting started with Intelligent Huddles™. I know you can do this! I'm here for you and I can't wait to hear about your success!

END NOTES

INTRODUCTION

1 - TheSalonBusiness.com: https://thesalonbusiness.com/are-hair-salons-profitable/

CHAPTER 1

1 - Bureau of labor and statistics: https://www.bls.gov/news.release/tenure.t06.htm

2 - Gallup: https://www.gallup.com/workplace/247391/fixable-problem-costs-businesses-trillion.aspx

3 - Gallup: https://www.gallup.com/workplace/247391/fixable-problem-costs-businesses-trillion.aspx

4 - Peakon Study: https://peakon.com/heartbeat/reports/the-employee-voice/

5 - William Kahn Study: https://www.talenteck.com/academic/Kahn-1990.pdf

6 - Creating We Institute: https://creatingwe.com/benchmark/the-company

CHAPTER 2

1 - HeartMath Institute: https://www.heartmath.org/research/science-of-the-heart/energetic-communication/

2 - Healthline: https://www.healthline.com/nutrition/gut-brain-connection#TOC_TITLE_HDR_2

3 - Chemical & Engineering News: https://cen.acs.org/biological-chemistry/microbiome/gut-might-modify-mind/97/i14

4 - Psychology Today: https://www.psychologytoday.com/us/blog/the-athletes-way/201211/the-neurochemicals-happiness

5 - Project Aristotle: https://rework.withgoogle.com/guides/understanding-team-effectiveness/steps/foster-psychological-safety/

6 - Very Well Mind: https://www.verywellmind.com/what-is-emotional-intelligence-2795423

7 - Project Aristotle: https://rework.withgoogle.com/guides/understanding-team-effectiveness/steps/foster-psychological-safety/

8 - Paul J. Zak Study: https://rework.withgoogle.com/blog/creating-a-high-trust-performance-culture/

9 - Paul J. Zak Study: https://rework.withgoogle.com/blog/creating-a-high-trust-performance-culture/

10 - Paul J. Zak Study: https://rework.withgoogle.com/blog/creating-a-high-trust-performance-culture/

11 - Hormone Health Network: https://www.hormone.org/your-health-and-hormones/glands-and-hormones-a-to-z/hormones/cortisol

12 - CI-Q for Coaches: https://ciq.wbecs.com/wp-content/uploads/2020/04/C-IQ-Conversational-Dashboard-with-Up-Down-Regulating-v2.pdf

13 - CI-Q for Coaches: https://ciq.wbecs.com/wp-content/uploads/2020/04/C-IQ-Conversational-Dashboard-with-Up-Down-Regulating-v2.pdf

End Notes

CHAPTER 3

1 - Harvard Business Review: https://hbr.org/2019/01/how-to-spend-way-less-time-on-email-every-day

2 - Wall Street Journal Online: https://www.wsj.com/articles/SB10001424127887324339204578173252223022388

CHAPTER 7

1 - Grant Thorton Research: https://www.grantthornton.com/library/articles/advisory/2019/return-on-culture/healthy-cultures-keep-score.aspx

2 - Grant Thorton Research: https://www.grantthornton.com/library/articles/advisory/2019/return-on-culture/healthy-cultures-keep-score.aspx

ABOUT THE AUTHOR

Andrea Hemmer

Andrea Hemmer is one of the most exciting, successful, and intellectual new leaders in the Salon and Beauty Industry.

Just as the economy was crashing in 2008, Andrea opened the Boise location of Lunatic Fringe. The salon thrived because of her deep curiosity and thoughtful study of neuroscience related to human behavior. What she discovered, was the success of the salon hinged on the emotional intelligence of the leadership as much as it did on the bottom line.

Andrea infused her neuroscience training in her every day interactions with her stylists. This thoughtful study of those around her helped her learn what actions strengthened the culture of the workplace, and the individuals as well. It was her commitment to open communication that made the largest impact on the salon. Andrea started each work day at the salon the same way, with a daily huddle.

Andrea now focuses on supporting other businesses and team leaders to implement her communication tools and systems in their own environment. Her program centers on building a foundation of self-awareness, mindfulness, and inner-evaluation to have the ability to adapt and pivot through rapid change. Andrea's gift for mentorship and her unique blending of neuroscience, mindfulness, and spirituality led her to create the groundbreaking program, Intelligent Huddles™.

IF YOU WOULD LIKE ANDREA TO WORK WITH YOU, OR YOUR ORGANIZATION, CONNECT WITH HER AT:

www.DreaHemmer.com

There, you will be able to contact Andrea for one-on-one leadership training, group training, or you can request for her to speak at your organization or event.

Don't forget, you can download many huddle resources by visiting www.dreahemmer.com/huddleresources.

Finally, if you enjoyed this book, it would be amazing if you would leave a review on the retailer site where you purchased *Intelligent Huddles*.

Thank you again for dedicating the time to read this book and I wish you all the success in the world!

Made in United States
North Haven, CT
05 November 2022